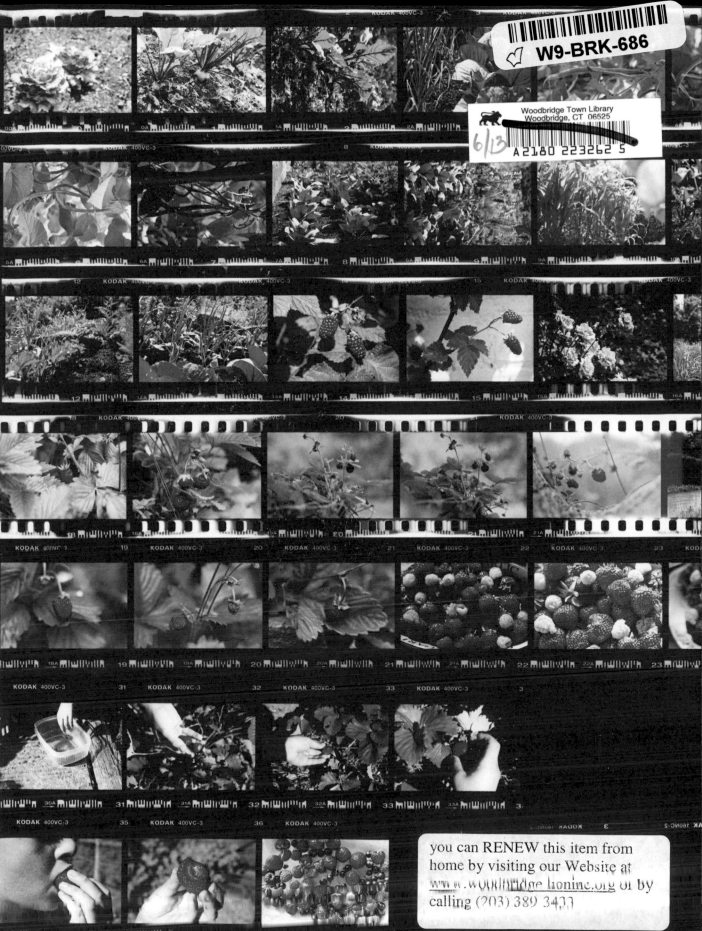

FOOD

MARY McCARTNEY
FOOD

STERLING EPICURE
New York

STERLING EPICURE
New York

An Imprint of Sterling Publishing
387 Park Avenue South
New York, NY 10016

First Sterling edition published in 2013

First published in Great Britain in 2012 by Chatto & Windus, Random House

Art direction and design by Jesse Holborn / Design Holborn

ISBN 978-1-4549-0726-8

Distributed in Canada by Sterling Publishing
℅ Canadian Manda Group, 165 Dufferin Street
Toronto, Ontario, Canada M6K 3H6

For information about custom editions, special sales, and premium and corporate purchases,
please contact Sterling Special Sales at 800-805-5489 or specialsales@sterlingpublishing.com.

Manufactured in China

2 4 6 8 10 9 7 5 3 1

www.sterlingpublishing.com

*Me and Mum, Scotland, 1971—and the beginning
of my journey with a passion for food.*

INTRODUCTION XVII

COOKING NOTES 1

BREAKFAST AND BRUNCH 9

SNACKS AND SANDWICHES 37

SOUPS, SALADS, AND STARTERS 61

MAINS 109

BASICS AND SIDES 155

DESSERTS AND BAKING 181

ACKNOWLEDGMENTS 227

INDEX 229

INTRODUCTION

have a confession to make. By profession I'm a photographer not a cook, but cooking is something I love to do. So I have been lucky enough to combine my two passions and have written and photographed almost everything in this book. By indulging both my great loves, I have found myself more immersed in this project than perhaps I thought possible when the idea for the book was taking shape, and I have loved the process. Getting the recipe right, cooking it, and then immediately photographing the result at home has made this a truly organic, cottage industry. A friend even jokingly suggested I buy a printing press for the next one!

My husband and our friends were the ones who first made me seriously consider writing my own cookbook—they're always asking me to write down my recipes and say that I seem to "magic it up" out of nowhere while chatting with them. But, really, I think my feel for vegetarian cooking is so ingrained that it has become second nature. Growing up in a vegetarian family and having Mum at the helm in the kitchen, encouraging us all to dive in, was the best education I could have asked for. My whole family are real foodies, because everything we ate as we grew up was simply delicious, and all of it was hassle-free, quick, and uncomplicated. As the years have gone by I have continued to cook as my mum did, constantly experimenting with different combinations of ingredients, flavors, and textures. I have added my own touches and refined the recipes over time. Up until now these have stayed in my head; I'm not disciplined at writing anything down, so often a meal will be made once—enjoyed—and then forgotten.

I suppose this is part of my motivation for embarking on this project. It has made me take the time to write down measurements and methods and really think about my earliest childhood food memories and inspirations.

I like uncomplicated cooking, so usually it needs to be kept quite simple and not too time-consuming. I enjoy cooking with friends and family around me; it's certainly a social activity for me. When friends come over I don't go overboard trying to concoct culinary masterpieces, but stick to my usual cooking style which is relaxed, straightforward, and stress-free—the empty plates at the end of a meal tell me they are happy!

I think our early experiences and memories of food determine so much of our approach to it as we get older. I was lucky enough to enjoy a very varied vegetarian diet, and so, for me, it wasn't limiting because there was always choice. My siblings and I were involved in the experience of cooking from a very early age. The kitchen was the center of the universe and Mum got us involved, helping cook and tasting . . . always tasting. Now with my own children, I try to get them involved. We discuss meals, recipe ideas, and flavor combinations, and I have found that it gives them a point of view and demystifies the process. The more involved they are, the more interested they become in food and cooking.

When we were young, Mum let us choose our favorite meal on our birthdays. I often chose her cream of tomato soup and fluffy quiche with a large mixed salad. And now I let my kids do the same. I want that tradition to continue and I hope that involving them shows them how varied and tasty a vegetarian diet can be. I have included their favorite recipes—fresh pesto, quiche, tomato sauce, chocolate chip cookies, pavlova, and many more—in this book, and these are recipes that they have started to make for me! I hope this book encourages you and your children to have a go, too.

Many of the recipes in this book can be adapted and tweaked to your own taste, and if certain ingredients are not available (due to seasonality or logistics), usually others can be substituted instead; you don't have to be a slave to the recipe.

Cooking has always been about a mixture of things for me: eclectic influences, places, tastes, and ingredients that together form my own view of food and how it all goes together. But, above all, two people in my life have provided the foundation for my cooking style.

My main cooking influence was my mother, Linda. She described herself as a peasant cook and had the ability to transform whatever she found in the pantry into delicious meals. Her style was pretty laid-back and low maintenance. Being an American, the basis of her cooking was quite traditional and therefore, so is mine; I guess I learned by osmosis. I love making hearty soups, stews, fluffy rising quiches, large chef's salads and baked macaroni and cheese. Mum also influenced my love of snacks; deep-filled New York deli-style sandwiches, grab bags to snack on during long journeys, filled with nuts, raisins and little chocolate pieces. One of my lasting memories of Mum is the two of us snacking on a tried and true favorite of hers—rye toast with crunchy peanut butter and jam . . . alongside a hot cup of our favorite English breakfast tea.

When I was growing up I spent lots of happy times cooking and chatting with my mother. During those times I soaked up her knowledge, and gained an understanding of how certain extra-simple ingredients or cooking techniques could transform an ordinary dish into something special.

Her love of food was infectious, but never precious. She never seemed to write anything down, a trick I inherited, but which made the creation of this book particularly testing! My dad has also played his part in developing my cooking style as he would encourage us to come up with ideas to fill the "hole" in a vegetarian's plate—like still having Sunday dinner and not feeling cheated while others dive into their roast beef.

From a more technical point of view, the other culinary influence in my life was my French/American step-grandmother, Monique. She had been brought up as a stickler for rules and technique. As a child I found her quite austere, but when I hit my early twenties we found cooking as a common interest, and I am glad I took the time to cook with her and learn from some of her teachings. She was very precise, and collected recipes and measured ingredients methodically. This was completely new to me. She taught me how to make and roll pastry, and she inspired my enduring love of baking. She even got me hooked on using an oven thermometer to ensure the oven was accurate and at the right heat.

These influences and memories are so warm and colorful, and they have informed the type of cook I have become. I love feeding friends and family, getting everyone around the table together to enjoy the banter around informal meals, and for me, the satisfaction of wiped-clean plates is worth the effort. There was nothing boring about food when I grew up, and now I just want to share some of this passion in the hope that you'll find vegetarian food as enticing, varied and delicious as I have all these years.

It has been a challenge balancing the desire to create something new and exciting with the rigor of writing down a new recipe. With that in mind, my wonderfully encouraging Aunt Louise bought me a beautiful wooden recipe box. Now when I make something new that is a success, and my husband despairs, wondering if I'll ever remember to make it again, I can write it down on a card and put it straight into the recipe box (well, most of the time!). This always makes me smile and raise a glass to my mum.

♡ Mary

Note from my mum on the fridge.

COOKING NOTES

AL DENTE PASTA AND VEGETABLES

I like pasta and most vegetables to be cooked "al dente"—an Italian expression meaning "to the bite" or "to the tooth"—so that they are still slightly firm and not too soggy. It's a good idea to taste the pasta or vegetable when you think it is almost ready—and take a bite. Basically, you want to feel a little resistance in the center.

BLIND BAKING

The recipes in this book that use pastry involve blind baking (pre-baking) the pastry shell before you put the filling in, because this is the best way to help prevent the bottom of the pie crust from becoming too soggy and doughy.

FREEZING

I often make too much and then freeze what we don't eat, so I've always got the good stuff ready in the freezer. Foodstuffs that freeze well are soups, vegetable stocks, gravy, shepherd's pie, lasagna, sauces, etc. I also like to have an emergency supply of bagels, bread, and milk. When freezing liquids, do not overfill containers, as liquid expands when frozen. Baked goods, such as cookies, muffins and cakes, freeze well too. There are foods that don't freeze well, such as vegetables with a high water content; for example, cucumber, cabbage, oranges, lettuce, celery, and onion. Egg-based sauces won't work that well either, but dairy products such as milk, butter and cream can be frozen. Over time, your freezer can become an Aladdin's cave of hidden treasures waiting for the right moment.

INGREDIENTS

• **VEGETARIAN CHEESES**: There is a wide variety of cheeses that are suitable for vegetarians, and they are now much more widely available in local shops and supermarkets. These cheeses are made without using animal rennet (animal rennet is not vegetarian, as it is an enzyme that comes from the stomachs of animals). Parmesan can sometimes be more difficult to find. BelGioioso does a great vegetarian Parmesan cheese (http://belgioioso. com) that can be bought in wedges (rather than the pre-grated stuff, which I find lacks taste), and it keeps well frozen for up to five months. If you cannot find Parmesan, then a good sharp hard cheese will substitute perfectly well.

INGREDIENTS

• **MEAT SUBSTITUTES:** I sometimes like to cook using vegetarian meat substitutes. The ground meat substitute works well added to sauces in recipes such as shepherd's pie, spaghetti bolognese, lasagna, and chili con carne. In the summer I like to barbecue vegetarian burgers and sausages with all the trimmings! These meat substitutes are now widely available in supermarkets and health food stores. There are available alternatives to most types of meat such as vegetarian sausages, burgers, ground meat, and chicken. These are often made using natural proteins from soy, wheat, and pea protein.

• **EGGS:** In all the recipes in this book, I recommend using large, free-range eggs (preferably organic, too), but if you use medium-sized ones I don't think it will cause any problems. I use free-range eggs rather than eggs produced by hens kept in cages in factory farms. The move to free-range eggs by many consumers has seen a huge positive change in suppliers replacing factory eggs with free-range. Let's keep up the pressure.

• **SUGAR:** I like to use natural granulated or superfine sugar. Unrefined (raw) cane sugar is a good alternative to bleached white refined sugar.

• **VANILLA:** These recipes use vanilla extract NOT vanilla flavoring. Vanilla extract is made by soaking vanilla beans in alcohol and water so that the flavor is infused into the liquid. It can be expensive, but keeps in the fridge for a long time while retaining its flavor.

• **VEGETABLE STOCK:** I have included a fresh vegetable stock recipe if you want to make your own. It can be kept in the fridge for up to 5 days, and it freezes well too. I also often use Marigold reduced-salt Swiss vegetable bouillon powder instead of fresh stock, which is available from online supermarkets and in health food stores

• **BAKING CHOCOLATE AND COCOA POWDER:** I like to use Green & Black's plain dark chocolate 70%, although there are several great-quality chocolate brands available. I think, for baking, as long as you stick to 70% cocoa content, then it should be fine.

• **SPELT and LIGHT SPELT FLOUR**: I have started to use organic stone-ground spelt flour in place of all-purpose flour (although either will do). Spelt flour is an ancient wheat variety which is meant to be easily digestible. Light spelt flour has been sifted from the coarse outer layers of the bran, and has a similar texture to all-purpose flour. You can turn both spelt and all-purpose flour into self-rising flour by adding 2 teaspoons of baking powder per every 2 cups of flour. The recipes in this book call for light spelt flour because it is closer to all-purpose flour than regular spelt flour.

BREAKFAST AND BRUNCH

FRUIT AND NUT GRANOLA

I always used to buy granola, until a friend showed me how easy and satisfying it is to make. What I love about it is that once you've made the syrup and measured the oats you can modify the other ingredients to your own taste, by using your own choice of nuts, seeds, and dried fruit (sticking roughly to the specified amounts for each ingredient). Or you can stick with this recipe, which I think is well balanced, and has a lovely roasted flavor. I love to serve this with a big spoonful of plain yogurt and some blueberries on top.

MAKES APPROX. 1½ pounds

INGREDIENTS

- 5 cups rolled oats, preferably old-fashioned (not instant) oats
- 10 brazil nuts, roughly chopped
- ⅓ cup sunflower seeds, roughly chopped
- ⅓ cup pumpkin seeds, roughly chopped
- 8 dried apricots, chopped
- ⅓ cup raisins
- ⅓ cup dried cranberries

For the syrup:
- 3 tablespoons sunflower or cooking oil
- 5½ tablespoons maple syrup
- 5½ tablespoons honey

METHOD

- Preheat the oven to 300°F. Line 2 baking sheets with parchment paper.
- In a large mixing bowl, combine the oats, brazil nuts, sunflower, and pumpkin seeds. Set this aside while you make the syrup.
- To make the syrup, pour the oil, maple syrup and honey into a small saucepan and heat gently until warm but not bubbling, stirring well until all the ingredients are mixed together. Take care not to let it bubble and overcook.
- Drizzle the syrup over the oats, nuts, and seeds, and mix together so that all the ingredients are lightly coated.
- Spread the mixture evenly over the 2 baking sheets, so that it is about ½ inch deep. Bake for 30–40 minutes, taking it out of the oven 2 times during baking to stir the granola and then return it to continue baking. When it's ready it should be evenly golden brown.
- Take the granola out of the oven and mix in the apricots, raisins, and cranberries.
- Set the granola aside to cool completely, then store in an airtight container and keep in a cool dry place until needed (stored like this, it will keep for 2–3 weeks).

FRUITY OMEGA SMOOTHIES

These smoothies are an easy and refreshing way of getting those essential omega oils into your diet. I like to use frozen strawberries—they last well and help to keep the smoothie nice and cold. You can buy omega oil in most supermarkets or health food stores.

STAWBERRY AND BANANA

MAKES 4

INGREDIENTS

· 2 bananas
· 8 frozen strawberries
· 1¾ cups fresh apple juice
· 2 tablespoons liquid Omega 3 6 9 oil

METHOD

· Peel the bananas, then break them in half or chop roughly into quarters before putting them in your blender. Add the frozen strawberries and then pour in the apple juice and omega oil. Blend until smooth, which should take about 1 minute.
· Pour the smoothie into glasses or cups, and serve immediately while it's still cold.

TROPICAL PINEAPPLE AND COCONUT

MAKES 4

INGREDIENTS

· ¼ fresh pineapple, peeled, cored, and cut into chunks (you can use canned if you don't have fresh, approx. 1 cup)
· ½ cup coconut milk
· 1¾ cups fresh orange juice
· 2 tablespoons liquid Omega 3 6 9 oil

METHOD

· Place all the ingredients in a blender and blend well, for about 1 minute, until smooth.
· Pour the smoothie into glasses or cups, and serve immediately.

GRANOLA BAR TO GO

This is my favorite guilt-free snack for breakfasts on the go, packed lunches or just to have in your bag for hungry moments. And, as it cooks, it fills your home with the wonderful smell of fresh home baking.

MAKES 12–14 PIECES

INGREDIENTS

- ¾ cup agave syrup
- 3 tablespoons butter
- 4 tablespoons vegetable or light olive oil
- ¼ teaspoon ground cinnamon
- 1 tablespoon vanilla extract
- 4 cups rolled oats
- 2 ¾ cups cornflakes
- ¾ cup whole almonds, coarsely chopped
- 16 dried apricots, coarsely chopped
- ⅔ cup dark or golden raisins
- 2 tablespoons sunflower seeds
- 2 tablespoons pumpkin seeds

METHOD

- Line a baking sheet (approx. 11 x 8 inches) with parchment paper. Preheat the oven to 350°F.
- In a large saucepan, gently simmer the agave syrup for about 4 minutes, to allow it to turn a bit syrupy (be careful, this is very hot). Take it off the heat and then add the butter and vegetable oil, stirring well until the butter has melted. Add the cinnamon and vanilla extract and then mix in the oats, cornflakes, almonds, apricots, raisins, sunflower, and pumpkin seeds. Stir well to ensure that all the ingredients are coated in the syrup.
- Spoon the granola mix onto the baking sheet and push it down firmly so that it's evenly packed on the sheet.
- Bake it in the oven for 15–20 minutes, until the top turns golden.
- Remove the granola from the oven and let it cool before lifting it out of the baking sheet, cutting it into pieces, and then peeling off the parchment.

BANANA MUFFINS

MAKES 10–12 MUFFINS

INGREDIENTS

- 2¼ cups all-purpose or light spelt flour
- 2 teaspoons baking powder
- ½ cup sugar, either raw superfine or granulated
- 1 large free-range egg
- 3 large or 4 medium ripe bananas, mashed well
- 1 teaspoon vanilla extract
- ½ cup sour cream or crème fraîche
- 7 tablespoons butter, melted

- 10–12 paper muffin liners

METHOD

- Preheat the oven to 350°F. Place the muffin liners into a 12-well non-stick muffin tin.
- Put all the ingredients into a large mixing bowl and beat together until well combined. You can use a food processor for this if preferred.
- Divide the batter equally in the lined muffin tin.
- Bake for 20 minutes, until the tops have turned golden and are just firm to the touch. I think these are best served warm—but they can be kept for about 3 days in an airtight container.

QUICK BREAKFAST BOWL

SERVES 1

INGREDIENTS

- ¼ cup muesli or granola
- 1 tablespoon flaxseeds
- ¼ cup plain live culture yogurt
- 1 medium banana, thinly sliced
- 2 tablespoons blueberries, or 4 sliced strawberries (or another seasonal fruit of your choice), chopped into bite-sized pieces (optional)
- 5 walnuts, broken into pieces
- 1 tablespoon honey or maple syrup

METHOD

- Spoon the muesli or granola into a large breakfast bowl, sprinkle the flaxseeds over the cereal, then spoon the yogurt on top. Arrange the banana, blueberries (or other fruit), and nuts over the top and, finally, drizzle the honey or maple syrup over the top. And it's ready!

FRENCH TOAST

One of my favorite weekend breakfast dishes, this is something I grew up eating, but didn't actually learn how to make until I was in my early 20s. I must have assumed it was more complicated to make than it really is. It's perfect as a satisfying special breakfast or brunch for family and friends when you have only a few eggs, milk, and some bread that's past its best in your pantry—suddenly these ingredients are transformed into an indulgent, golden delight when a generous drizzle of pure maple syrup is poured over the top. My dad grew up calling it "eggy bread," and his family never ate it sweet with maple syrup; instead they had tomato ketchup on the side. You can experiment by using different types of bread, although I usually stick to thickly sliced wholegrain, organic white, or multigrain bread that's not too fresh or soft. And you can vary the flavor, if you like, by adding a pinch of ground cinnamon, or a teaspoon of vanilla extract, or orange zest to the eggy mix.

SERVES 4

INGREDIENTS

· 3 large, free-range eggs
· 2½ cups milk
· butter, for frying
· 8 slices bread, preferably thick-sliced and a couple of days old
· pure maple syrup, to pour on top

METHOD

· In a wide, shallow bowl (wide enough to fit a slice of bread), beat the eggs and milk together until well blended.
· Heat a large non-stick frying pan over medium-high heat. When it is hot, add a small amount of butter and tilt it around the pan to melt and lightly cover the pan base.
· Dip the bread, 1 slice at a time, into the mixture and allow it to soak up some of the eggy milk on both sides (but don't let it get too soggy).
· Gently place as many slices of the soaked bread into the hot pan as will comfortably fit, and fry for a couple of minutes on each side, using a slotted (rubber or plastic) spatula to flip the bread. Fry until a deep golden brown on both sides.
· Serve immediately with maple syrup drizzled over the top, or you can make this in batches, keeping some slices warm in the oven at a low temperature while you soak and fry the remaining pieces.

RHUBARB COMPOTE

SERVES APPROX. 4

INGREDIENTS

- 14 ounces rhubarb stalks, trimmed
- ¼ cup sugar or agave syrup
- juice of 1 orange

METHOD

- Rinse the rhubarb stalks and cut them into ¾ inch pieces. Put the rhubarb into a medium saucepan, add the sugar or syrup and pour in the freshly squeezed orange juice.
- Simmer gently over medium heat for about 8–10 minutes, until the rhubarb is cooked through but still holds its shape. Transfer to a bowl. Once cooled, it can be kept in the fridge for up to 3 days.

HEARTY PORRIDGE

SERVES 2–3

INGREDIENTS

- 1 cup rolled oats
- 1 ¼ cups milk or soy milk
- 1 ¼ cups water
- 1 tablespoon flaxseeds
- 1 tablespoon mixed sunflower and pumpkin seeds, finely chopped
- honey or maple syrup (approx. 1 tablespoon per bowl), for drizzling on top
- chopped seasonal fruit or berries, for sprinkling on top (optional)

METHOD

- Place the oats in a medium saucepan and mix in the milk and water. Bring to the boil and gently simmer for 5–10 minutes, stirring often to keep the porridge from sticking to the pan.
- Once the porridge is cooked, take the pan off the heat and add the flaxseeds and the sunflower/pumpkin seed mix. Stir well and pour into breakfast bowls.
- Drizzle honey or maple syrup over the porridge.
- Serve hot, topped with some chopped fruit or berries, if you like.

BREAKFAST PANCAKES

Many of my favorite memories of Mum involve food—cooking together and then chatting as we ate. One morning, we were both home alone so we decided to cook blueberry pancakes, poured a generous amount of maple syrup over them, then got back into bed to eat and watched the classic film La Dolce Vita. *This recipe is for classic breakfast pancakes, but you can add a handful or two of blueberries to the batter if you like.*

MAKES ABOUT 16 PANCAKES

INGREDIENTS

- 1 cup self-rising flour
- 1 teaspoon baking powder
- 2 large, free-range eggs
- ¾ cup milk
- 2 teaspoons vegetable, sunflower, or olive oil
- 2 teaspoons butter
- maple syrup, to pour on top

METHOD

- Sift the flour and baking powder into a medium/large mixing bowl or food processor. Make a well in the center of the flour, crack the eggs into it and beat well. Slowly pour in the milk, beating constantly (so you don't get lumps). Keep beating until all the milk is mixed in and the batter is a smooth, creamy consistency—it should be light with a few air bubbles. Stir in the oil.
- When the pancake batter is ready, heat a large, non-stick frying pan over medium heat and melt in the butter.
- Check that the pan is hot enough to cook the pancakes by dropping a tiny amount of the batter into the pan—if it sizzles, the pan's ready.
- Now pour the batter into the pan, 1 tablespoon at a time, and make pancakes about 2½ inches in diameter—cooking batches of 4 if the frying pan size allows.
- When you notice small bubbles appearing on the surface, use a rubber spatula to slightly lift the edges of the pancakes to check that the underside has turned golden brown. Then flip them over and cook the other side until that, too, is golden brown and cooked through.
- Slide the pancakes onto plates and serve hot with maple syrup poured on top.

SAUCY MUSHROOMS AND TOMATOES ON TOAST

I love these for a weekend breakfast or brunch. They are really tasty and satisfying, and because they are broiled, and not fried, you can feel quite self-righteous about the whole thing. Great with scrambled eggs.

SERVES 2

INGREDIENTS

- 10 large button mushrooms
- 8 cherry tomatoes or 2 medium tomatoes
- 2 tablespoons light olive oil
- 2 tablespoons soy sauce
- 3 sprigs thyme, rinsed and leaves removed, or 1 teaspoon dried thyme or mixed herbs
- 2 cloves garlic, finely chopped, or 1 teaspoon granulated garlic
- 2–4 slices bread
- butter, for the toast
- black pepper, to taste

METHOD

- Heat the broiler to high.
- Clean off any gritty bits from the mushrooms, trim the stems and arrange the mushrooms on a baking sheet. Cut the tomatoes in half and arrange them on the sheet with the mushrooms.
- Drizzle the olive oil and soy sauce evenly over the mushrooms and tomatoes. Sprinkle the herbs and chopped garlic over the vegetables.
- Place the sheet under the broiler to cook for 8–10 minutes, watching them closely until the mushrooms and tomatoes are cooked through and the juices are bubbling.
- In the meantime toast and butter the bread.
- When they're ready, arrange the mushrooms and tomatoes on the toast, and add a grind or two of black pepper.

DEEP-FILLED OMELETTE

My mum would often make this omelette to eat at brunch on the weekends, but I sometimes make it for a quick supper too. I love the thick brightly colored tomato filling—it makes it really special and satisfying. It's perfect served with freshly buttered multigrain toast.

SERVES 2

INGREDIENTS

- 2 tablespoons vegetable or light olive oil
- 2 medium onions, thinly sliced
- I stalk celery, trimmed and finely chopped (optional)
- 4 cremini or button mushrooms, thinly sliced
- 14.5 ounce can chopped tomatoes
- I teaspoon dried herbs (such as sage, parsley or thyme) or I tablespoon fresh
- sea salt and black pepper, to taste
- 4 large, free-range eggs
- I tablespoon butter
- 2 ounces sharp Cheddar, grated (optional)

METHOD

- To make the filling, heat the oil in a medium or large frying pan over medium heat, then add the onion slices and sauté for 5 minutes. Add the celery and cook gently for 2 minutes more, stirring frequently. Mix in the mushrooms and sauté for another 5–8 minutes, until the juice from the mushrooms has evaporated and the mushrooms start to turn golden brown.
- Mix in the tomatoes and the herbs, and season with sea salt and black pepper. Simmer gently for 20 minutes, checking and stirring often. The sauce should reduce down and thicken nicely. Set aside while you make the omelette.
- Crack the eggs into a mixing bowl and beat them well. In a large frying pan, melt the butter over medium-high heat.
- Once the pan and butter are hot, but not burning, pour in the eggs and swirl them around the base of the pan to coat it evenly. Season with black pepper and sprinkle the cheese (if using) over the eggs. Allow the eggs to cook through and the edges and bottom of the omelette to turn golden brown. You can finish cooking it under the broiler if necessary. Once it's cooked, take the pan off the heat and spoon the warm tomato mixture onto one half of the omelette. Fold the opposite side over the filling and cut it in half. Slide onto 2 plates.
- Serve hot.

SNACKS AND SANDWICHES

HUMMUS, AVOCADO AND CHILI JAM SANDWICH

This sandwich combination is so addictive, it makes my mouth water just looking at the recipe.

SERVES 1

INGREDIENTS

· 2 slices of sandwich bread, preferably a seeded or wholegrain loaf
· 2 tablespoons hummus
· 1 tablespoon chili pepper jam
· ½ Hass avocado, peeled, pitted and thinly sliced
· squeeze of lemon juice
· small handful green salad leaves
· sea salt and black pepper, to taste

METHOD

· Spread the 2 slices of bread with 1 tablespoon each of hummus. Spread the chili jam on top of 1 slice, and then arrange a layer of avocado slices on top of that. Squeeze a little lemon juice over the avocado, then layer the greens on top and season with a little sea salt and black pepper. Sandwich the other slice of hummus-coated bread on top, and eat immediately. Yum.

PAN-FRIED
TORTILLA SANDWICH

The melty cheese, avocado, and chili kick make this one of my favorite lunchtime snacks. It's great served with a salad, such as the Sprout and Carrot Salad on p. 85. It is simple to make, and so comforting to eat.

SERVES 1

INGREDIENTS

- 2 corn or flour tortillas (approx. 7 inches)
- 6 slices sharp cheese, such as goat Cheddar or sharp Cheddar (approx. 3 ounces)
- ½ ripe Hass avocado, peeled, pitted, and cut into ⅓ inch slices
- 1 scallion, trimmed and finely chopped
- ½ fresh red chili, chopped, or ¼ teaspoon dried chili flakes
- squeeze of fresh lime juice (approx. ½ teaspoon)
- pinch sea salt and freshly ground black pepper, to taste

METHOD

- Heat a medium non-stick frying pan over medium heat and lay in 1 tortilla. Next, place the cheese slices evenly across the tortilla, then the avocado slices, followed by the scallion, chili, and finally, a squeeze of lime juice, sea salt, and black pepper. Then lay the second tortilla on top to form your sandwich.
- Once the underside of the tortilla sandwich is lightly browned, flip it over carefully. Allow the second side to cook through for a minute or until the cheese has melted. Eat hot.

PAN-FRIED CHEESE, TOMATO AND ONION SANDWICH

This recipe makes one sandwich—simple, quick, melty, and indulgent. I love it served with coleslaw.

SERVES I

INGREDIENTS

- 2 slices sandwich bread
- I tablespoon butter
- 6 slices cheese, such as sharp Cheddar, goat Cheddar, or Gouda
- 2 thin slices red onion
- 4 thin slices ripe tomato
- freshly ground black pepper, to taste

METHOD

- Butter both slices of bread and lay them, butter-side down, on a chopping board. Lay the cheese on one of the slices of bread (unbuttered side), then top with the onion, tomato, and black pepper. Finally, place the second piece of bread, butter-side up, on top.
- Heat a medium frying pan over medium-high heat. When the pan is hot place the sandwich, butter-side down, in the pan. Fry on one side until it's golden brown, about 2 minutes, occasionally pushing down the sandwich to help melt the cheese, then flip the sandwich over and fry on the second side for another couple of minutes until golden brown and the cheese has melted.

Peanut butter, sliced banana and honey on toast.

Mature cheddar and coleslaw on seeded bread.

Toasted bagel with Marmite and hummus.

Falafel, hummus, chopped tomato and fresh mint, with a squeeze of lemon.

Sliced avocado, grated carrot, alfalfa sprouts and thousand island dressing.

Club sandwich: sliced boiled egg, fried halloumi, sliced red onion, tomato lettuce, mayo, mustard.

Soft goats cheese, fresh basil leaves, sliced marinated artichoke, sundried tomato, black pepper.

Veggi burger, cheese, crisp lettuce, sliced gherkin, tomato ketchup, mayo, mustard.

WARM EGGPLANT SANDWICH

This is a warm, comforting sandwich that I particularly enjoy on a rainy afternoon; it really has the ability to cheer me up when it is grey. The chili flakes provide optional extra heat, if you are in the mood for a bit of spice. And a tasty alternative to the feta cheese is a mix of 2 tablespoons of tahini paste with 1 tablespoon of lemon juice—drizzle this over the warm eggplant filling once it is spooned onto the bread.

SERVES 2

INGREDIENTS

· 2 tablespoons light olive oil
· I medium onion, thinly sliced
· I medium eggplant, cut into bite-sized cubes
· ½ teaspoon soy sauce
· 6 sundried tomatoes, chopped
· I teaspoon finely chopped fresh parsley or oregano, or ½ teaspoon dried oregano
· small pinch dried chili flakes (optional)
· French bread or crusty rolls
· butter, for the bread
· 3 ounces crumbled feta cheese
· squeeze of fresh lemon juice (½ lemon)
· pinch sea salt
· black pepper, to taste

METHOD

· Preheat the oven to 325°F.
· Heat the oil in a medium frying pan over medium heat, then add the onion and fry for 5 minutes. Add the eggplant pieces and fry for 5–8 minutes more, until they turn a golden brown. Mix in the soy sauce, sundried tomatoes, herbs, and the chili flakes, and cook until warmed through.
· Slice the French bread or crusty rolls down the middle and lightly butter the bread. Wrap in aluminum foil and warm in the oven for IO minutes.
· Spoon the eggplant mixture onto the bread, then crumble the feta cheese over it, followed by a squeeze of lemon juice. Season with a small pinch of sea salt and a grind of black pepper. Serve hot.

POPCORN

Freshly popped corn is a favorite snack from my childhood. I can still remember the anticipation of waiting for the corn to start popping. It felt like a lifetime and just when I thought it wasn't going to work, pop pop pop, it would go crazy! The gentle smell of popped corn would fill the kitchen. I like to eat it the classic American way with a little melted butter drizzled over the top, but I have included a sweet option here, too. It's the perfect snack to eat when you're watching a movie at home.

SERVES 2–4

INGREDIENTS

To pop the corn:
· 1 teaspoon sunflower, vegetable, or olive oil
· ¾ cup popping corn

Buttery option:
· 3 tablespoons salted butter

Sweet option:
· 3 tablespoons salted butter
· 3 tablespoons soft brown sugar
· 3 tablespoons golden syrup, honey, or maple syrup

METHOD

· Use a large, heavy-bottomed saucepan with a lid (a see-through lid is best so you can see how the corn is popping).
· Put the oil in the pan over medium heat. Once the oil is hot and rippling (near smoking point), pour in the popcorn kernels and immediately put the lid on the pan, so you don't let the heat out. Shake the pan gently so that the corn kernels don't burn on the bottom of the pan.
· Wait until you hear the corn start to pop—it's only a short wait, so keep shaking the pan often so that the corn moves around and doesn't burn. When you hear the popping really slow down, take the pan off the heat and set it aside for a minute. Then pour the popped corn into a large mixing bowl. Toss together well with your preferred topping and eat immediately.

· Buttery option: Melt the butter in a small saucepan and drizzle it over the popped corn. Toss well.

· Sweet option: Melt the butter in a small saucepan, stir in the brown sugar and golden syrup until melted together. Pour the topping over your popped corn and toss well to evenly coat it.

DELUXE
EGG SALAD

I used to love it when Mum made egg salad, because I could wipe any leftovers from the bowl with a piece of soft, fresh, buttered bread. So it has remained a favorite for me. I like this served in a soft seeded roll, or as a generous filling for a toasted bagel. And I also love it as an open-faced sandwich, just spread on a piece of toast, with a thin slice of fresh tomato on top.

MAKES 4–6 SANDWICHES, depending how much filling you like to stuff in!

INGREDIENTS

- 6 large, free-range eggs, hard-boiled
- I tablespoon red onion or scallions, finely chopped
- I stalk celery, trimmed and finely chopped
- 4 heaped tablespoons mayonnaise
- I heaped teaspoon Dijon mustard (wholegrain or smooth)
- I teaspoon pickle relish (optional)
- sea salt and black pepper, to taste

METHOD

- Remove the shells from the hard-boiled eggs and mash them with a fork in a medium mixing bowl.
- Mix in the chopped onion and celery. Then stir in the mayonnaise, mustard, and relish (if using) and mix together well. Season with sea salt and black pepper.

HALOUMI BBQ SKEWERS

These skewers are so quick and tasty. Grilled haloumi cheese is great with just about anything, but it really comes to life with this tangy BBQ sauce. I like to serve these with steamed rice or new potatoes.

SERVES 4

INGREDIENTS

- ½ recipe **BBQ Sauce** (see p. 168)
- 2 small or medium onions or 8 small shallots
- 2 red peppers
- 2 medium zucchini
- 7 ounces haloumi cheese

- 8 pre-soaked wooden or metal skewers

METHOD

- Make a half quantity of the BBQ Sauce on page 168.
- Peel the onions and chop into quarters lengthwise through the root (if using shallots, just peel). Remove the seeds from the peppers and discard, and cut into 8 pieces. Next, cut the zucchini and haloumi cheese into 8 pieces.
- Prepare the skewers by alternating the chunks of haloumi with the peppers, onions, or shallots, and zucchini; 2 pieces of each ingredient per skewer. Brush the assembled skewers with a generous amount of the BBQ sauce on all sides.
- To cook, place the skewers under a hot broiler for about 10–12 minutes, turning often, until cooked and golden.
- Alternatively you can cook them in the oven at 350°F for 10–12 minutes. Or grill them on a preheated gas grill or barbecue.

GUACAMOLE

This is a dip that my mum loved to make and it remains one of my favorites. I adore it—it's bright and satisfying and quick to put together. It's more than just a dip to serve with tortilla chips or carrot sticks—I also find it irresistible spooned alongside a sandwich or onto a burrito, or dolloped onto a salad of mixed greens. It's also tasty spread on top of a veggie burger. If you like cilantro, then a tablespoon of the chopped herb stirred in works well too.

SERVES 2

INGREDIENTS

- 2 Hass avocados, halved and pitted
- I medium ripe tomato, finely chopped
- I small red chili, seeded and finely chopped, or 2 tablespoons chopped pickled jalapeños (from a jar) or dash Tabasco sauce
- I clove garlic, finely chopped
- juice of 2 limes (approx. 3 tablespoons)
- pinch sea salt and freshly ground black pepper, to taste

METHOD

- Scoop the avocado flesh out of the halves into a medium mixing bowl. Mash well with a fork and then stir in the chopped tomato, chili (or jalapeño or Tabasco), garlic, and lime juice. Season with sea salt and freshly ground black pepper.

JALAPEÑO TOSTADA

This is such a tasty snack and so quick and simple to make. The recipe is inspired by the cheese tostadas we used to eat at a family-favorite Mexican restaurant when I was growing up. I often make these for a super-quick supper and eat them with an Avocado Salad (see p. 84) on the side.

SERVES 1

INGREDIENTS

· 1 corn or flour tortilla (approx. 7 inches)
· 6 slices cheese, such as Monterey Jack or goat Cheddar (approx. 3 ounces)
· 2 tablespoons chopped pickled jalapeños (from a jar) or fresh green chilies

METHOD

· Preheat the broiler to medium. Line a baking sheet with aluminum foil.
· Place the tortilla on the baking sheet. Lay the cheese on top of the tortilla, leaving a $\frac{1}{3}$-inch border around the outer edge of the tortilla so that when the cheese goes under the broiler it melts up to, but not over, the edge.
· Sprinkle the jalapeños (or chilies) over the cheese. Now place the tostada under the broiler for a couple of minutes, until the cheese is bubbly and fully melted. Serve immediately.

SOUPS, SALADS, AND STARTERS

ROASTED BUTTERNUT SQUASH AND ROSEMARY SOUP

Roasting the butternut squash and the rosemary together first adds a luxurious aromatic twist to this delicious soup.

SERVES 4

INGREDIENTS

- I butternut squash
- 2 tablespoons light olive oil, plus more for drizzling over the squash
- 2 large sprigs fresh rosemary
- 2 medium onions, finely chopped
- 2 stalks celery, trimmed and chopped
- I medium carrot, chopped
- pinch (¼ teaspoon) chili flakes (optional)
- 3 ⅓ cups vegetable stock
- sea salt and black pepper, to taste
- 2 tablespoons crème fraîche or sour cream, plus more for serving (optional)

METHOD

- Preheat the oven to 325°F.
- Slice the butternut squash in half lengthwise, scoop out and discard the seeds and put both halves on a baking sheet. Drizzle some olive oil over the squash and lay the rosemary sprigs in the hollow of each squash half. Bake for 45 minutes. Allow the squash to cool slightly, discard the woody rosemary sprigs but keep the leaves, then peel off the outer skin of the squash and chop the flesh into cubes.
- In a large saucepan, over medium heat, sauté the onions, celery, and carrots in the oil for about 5 minutes. Stir in the squash pieces and the chili flakes, if using, and then pour in the vegetable stock; simmer gently for 15 minutes. Season with freshly ground black pepper and a little sea salt.
- When the mixture has cooled slightly, ladle it into a blender (or use a handheld blender). Mix in the crème fraîche or sour cream and blend until smooth.
- Pour the soup back into the saucepan, heat through, and serve topped with a dollop of crème fraîche or some Herby Croutons (see p. 160).

HEARTY QUINOA AND WHITE BEAN SOUP

This is a warming and very satisfying soup. I like to use quinoa because it's a really nutritious superfood that provides a great source of protein. The grainy texture helps make this soup filling enough to provide a meal in itself.

SERVES APPROX. 6

INGREDIENTS

- 4 tablespoons light olive oil
- 2 medium onions, finely chopped
- 2 large carrots, finely chopped
- 2 stalks celery, trimmed and diced
- 15 ounce can white beans (such as cannellini)
- 2 cloves garlic, finely chopped
- 14.5 ounce can chopped tomatoes
- 6 cups vegetable stock
- ⅓ cup quinoa
- ¼ cup chopped fresh parsley
- 1 tablespoon fresh oregano, rosemary, or thyme, chopped
- 1 bay leaf
- sea salt and black pepper, to taste

METHOD

- Heat the oil in a large, heavy-bottomed saucepan over medium heat. Add the onions, carrots, and celery and sauté for 5 minutes. Then add the beans and garlic and sauté for a couple of minutes more.
- Stir in the chopped tomatoes and vegetable stock, and simmer for 20 minutes.
- Finally, add the quinoa, parsley, oregano, or other herbs and the bay leaf, and cook for 12–15 minutes, to allow the quinoa to cook through. Season with sea salt and black pepper.

EASY-PEASY SOUP

This soup is a colorful vibrant green. It is really quick to make and uses frozen peas, so it's a great option when you're running low on fresh green vegetables, and yet the end result is a wonderfully tasty, sweet pea soup. Lovely served hot with crusty buttered bread.

SERVES 4

INGREDIENTS

· 2 tablespoons vegetable or light olive oil
· I leek, trimmed, washed, and finely chopped
· 2 medium onions, finely chopped
· 3 cloves garlic, finely chopped
· 2 medium potatoes, cut into small cubes
· 2I ounce bag frozen peas
· 3¾ cups vegetable stock
· I teaspoon dried mixed herbs, or I tablespoon chopped fresh parsley
· ¾ cup crème fraîche
· black pepper, to taste

METHOD

· In a medium heavy-bottomed saucepan, heat the oil over medium heat, then add the leek, onions, and garlic and gently fry them for about 5 minutes. Add the cubes of potatoes and the frozen peas, stir well and fry for about 2 minutes. Now pour in the vegetable stock and add the herbs. Stir well and simmer gently for I5 minutes.
· Leave this to cool just a little and then purée, using either a jar blender or a hand blender in the saucepan. Stir in the crème fraîche and a pinch of black pepper.

LIP-SMACKING MINESTRONE

I have always been a big fan of minestrone—the chunky texture and the hearty ingredients are so flavorful and comforting. You can have it as a lunch or starter, but it's filling enough to make a light supper too. I make a big batch and eat it throughout the week.

It's also a very versatile dish; you can mix and match vegetables that are in season and therefore make it slightly different according to what you have in your fridge and what you are in the mood for. The pasta is an optional extra as you might prefer a lighter soup. I find that kids love the little pasta stars. And, if basil is in season, it's nice to add a handful of roughly torn basil leaves to the soup in the last 10 minutes of cooking.

This soup is great on its own, topped with lots of grated Parmesan, or with garlic bread, or a sandwich to dip in it, or with buttered fresh bread . . . Yum, this is making me hungry!

SERVES 4–6

INGREDIENTS

- 3 tablespoons vegetable or light olive oil
- 1 medium onion, finely chopped
- 1 medium leek, trimmed, washed, and finely chopped
- 2 stalks celery, trimmed and finely chopped
- 2 medium to large carrots, finely chopped
- 14.5 ounce can chopped tomatoes
- 2 cloves garlic, finely chopped
- 1 quart vegetable stock
- 5 ounces (about 2 cups) green cabbage, grated or finely chopped
- 1 tablespoon fresh parsley, chopped
- 2 teaspoons fresh oregano, chopped
- 1 bay leaf
- 1 tablespoon tomato paste
- ¼ cup frozen peas or peeled fava beans
- ½ cup dried small macaroni, or ½ cup pasta stars pasta, or ½ cup broken up spaghetti (optional)
- sea salt and black pepper, to taste
- grated Parmesan or other hard cheese, to serve

METHOD

- Heat the olive oil in a large, heavy-bottomed saucepan over medium heat, then add the chopped onion, leek, celery, and carrots, stirring well, and cook for a couple of minutes, to allow the flavors of the vegetables to release.
- Stir in the chopped tomatoes and the garlic, then cover and simmer for 15 minutes, checking and stirring often. Pour in the vegetable stock, then add the cabbage, herbs, and the bay leaf, and mix in the tomato paste. Bring to a boil, reduce the heat, and let it simmer for 15 minutes.
- Add the frozen peas or broad beans and pasta and continue to simmer gently for a further 15 minutes. Add more stock if it's too thick. Taste, and season with sea salt (only if it needs it, as the stock may be salty enough) and ground black pepper. Ladle generously into soup bowls and sprinkle grated Parmesan cheese over the top.

MUST-HAVE CREAMY TOMATO SOUP

One of my favorite meals has always been a bowl of hot tomato soup eaten with a grilled cheese sandwich; it's like medicine to me—and pretty much guaranteed to cheer me up.

SERVES 4

INGREDIENTS

- 3 tablespoons light olive oil
- 3 medium onions, finely chopped
- 2 stalks celery, trimmed and chopped
- 2 cloves garlic, finely chopped
- 6 ripe tomatoes, blanched, peeled, and chopped
- 28 ounce can diced tomatoes
- ¾ cup vegetable stock
- I tablespoon tomato paste
- I tablespoon each chopped fresh rosemary leaves and sage, or ⅓ cup roughly chopped basil
- ¾ cup half-and-half, soy creamer, or crème fraîche
- sea salt and black pepper, to taste

METHOD

- Heat the oil over medium heat In a large, heavy-bottomed saucepan. Add the onions and celery and sauté for 10 minutes, then stir in the garlic and continue to sauté for a couple more minutes. Stir in the chopped fresh tomatoes.
- Stir in the canned tomatoes, vegetable stock, and the tomato paste. Let this mixture simmer gently for 12–15 minutes. Then mix in the herbs and take off the heat.
- Stir in the cream (or crème fraîche). Now season with a large pinch of sea salt and some freshly ground black pepper. Heat through until hot enough to serve.

LIGHTNING LENTIL SOUP

As the title implies, this is a quick soup that delivers on flavor and is also very satisfying. I find it's a great way to get the kids to eat lentils without complaining. This is best served hot with some garlic bread for dipping.

SERVES 4

INGREDIENTS

- 2 tablespoons light olive oil
- 3 medium onions, finely chopped
- 2 medium carrots, finely chopped
- 2 stalks celery, trimmed and finely chopped
- 14.5 ounce can cooked green lentils, preferably organic, drained
- ¼ teaspoon ground cumin
- 1½ teaspoons tomato paste
- 2½ cups vegetable stock
- freshly ground black pepper, to taste
- pinch chili flakes (optional)

METHOD

- Gently heat the oil over medium heat in a medium heavy-bottomed saucepan, and then add the chopped onions, carrots, and celery. Sauté for 3–4 minutes to allow the vegetables to start cooking and release their flavors. Add the drained can of lentils and stir together well.
- Stir in the cumin and tomato paste and heat through. Pour in the vegetable stock and allow the soup to simmer gently for 15 minutes.
- Let it cool slightly, then transfer the soup to a blender and whizz for about 15 seconds (or use a hand blender in the saucepan).
- Transfer the puréed soup back to the saucepan and heat it up again. Add a fresh grinding of black pepper, and a pinch of chili flakes if you want an extra kick.
- If you prefer a chunky soup, then do not blend.

LEEK, ZUCCHINI AND WHITE BEAN SOUP

I love the subtle blend of flavors in this soup. If I don't have any zucchini, I sometimes use green beans instead and that works really well too.

SERVES APPROX. 4

INGREDIENTS

- 2 tablespoons vegetable or light olive oil
- 2 medium leeks, trimmed, washed, and finely chopped
- 2 medium zucchini (approx. 14 ounces), finely diced
- 1 stalk celery, trimmed and finely chopped
- 15 ounce can white beans (such as cannellini)
- 3 ⅓ cups vegetable stock
- ½ teaspoon dried mixed herbs

METHOD

- Heat the oil over medium heat in a large saucepan and gently fry the leeks until they are soft and golden, which should take about 7 minutes. Stir in the zucchini, celery, and white beans, and fry for another 4 minutes or so.
- Pour in the vegetable stock and add the herbs, mixing well. Cover and simmer gently for 15 minutes.
- Allow the soup to cool slightly and then purée in a blender, or use a hand blender in the saucepan (or you can serve this chunky, depending on your preference). Pour the soup back into saucepan to reheat and then pour into bowls. It's good topped with the Herby Croutons (see p. 160).

EGGPLANT WRAPS

These wraps work well as a dinner party dish—either as a starter or as a main course with side dishes, such as warm potato salad or sautéed leeks with zucchini, alongside. You can assemble them beforehand and then bake them when your guests arrive, making for a more relaxing evening for you.

SERVES 4 (4 wraps per person)

INGREDIENTS

- 2 medium/large eggplants
- 2 tablespoons sunflower oil or light olive oil
- 1 tablespoon dried mixed herbs
- 14 ounces spinach
- 16 sundried tomato pieces, marinated in olive oil
- 3 tablespoons pine nuts, lightly toasted in a hot frying pan (no oil needed)
- 5 ounces sharp Cheddar, cut into 16 slices
- pinch sea salt
- black pepper, to taste

METHOD

- Preheat the oven to 350°F. You will need a large non-stick baking sheet.
- Cut the woody top off each eggplant and discard. Slice each eggplant lengthwise into 8 pieces (16 in all) about ½ inch thick.
- Mix the oil and the herbs together in a small bowl or cup. Lightly brush each slice of eggplant with the herby oil on both sides. Heat a large frying pan over medium heat and lay as many pieces of the eggplant in the pan as will comfortably fit. Fry each side until golden brown and softened, which should be about 3 minutes per side. When all the slices are cooked, set them aside.
- Wash the spinach well in cold running water, then toss it in a hot medium saucepan (using just the water that is clinging to the leaves) until wilted, and drain off the excess liquid.
- Now, assemble each wrap by taking 1 slice of the cooked eggplant and placing a little of the wilted spinach on one side. Then lay a piece of sundried tomato on top, sprinkle a few toasted pine nuts over it, and top with a slice of Cheddar. Fold the eggplant over to form the wrap, then place it on a large non-stick baking sheet.
- Repeat this until all 16 wraps are assembled and placed side by side on the baking sheet. Sprinkle with a pinch of sea salt and a grind of fresh black pepper.
- Bake in the oven for 15 minutes, until the cheese has melted and is bubbling, and serve immediately.

CORN FRITTERS

These fritters make a great starter or lunch. They work really well with various different sauces and dips, such as a spoonful of Guacamole on the side (see p. 53 for a recipe), or with sweet chili dipping sauce, or even a yogurt and cucumber dip. I like to use fresh chilies, but a pinch of dried chili flakes works well, too. When I am making these for kids, or friends that don't like spice, I just leave out the chili.

SERVES 4 (Makes about 12 3 inch fritters)

INGREDIENTS

- I cup all-purpose or light spelt flour
- ½ teaspoon baking powder
- 2 large, free-range eggs, beaten
- ⅓ cup milk
- 2 cups corn kernels, cut fresh off the cob
  (or frozen corn, thawed, or canned corn, drained)
- I clove garlic, finely chopped
- I red chili, seeded and finely chopped (optional)
- 2 scallions, trimmed and finely chopped
- I tablespoon fresh parsley or cilantro, chopped
- sea salt and black pepper, to taste
- I to 2 tablespoons vegetable or light olive oil for
  frying the fritters

For the dipping sauce:
- 6 tablespoons plain yogurt
- ½ small fresh red chili, finely chopped
- I tablespoon fresh parsley or cilantro, finely
  chopped
- I tablespoon chili pepper jam or sweet chili sauce
- ½ teaspoon freshly squeezed lemon juice

METHOD

- In a medium mixing bowl stir the flour and baking powder together, then gradually stir in the beaten eggs and milk. Mix well to form a smooth batter.
- Stir in the corn, garlic, chili (if using), scallions, and herbs, and mix the ingredients well so that they are coated in the batter. Season with salt and pepper.
- Heat the vegetable oil in a large non-stick frying pan until it is hot. You can test this by dropping a tiny bit of the batter into the pan—you should hear it sizzle when it hits the pan.
- Spoon in a tablespoon of the mixture for each fritter, leaving space between them so that they don't stick together (you may need to do this in batches). Pat each fritter down a bit so it's flatter and easy to cook on both sides. Fry until golden brown and then turn it over to brown the other side. This should take about 2 minutes per side. Repeat this process until all the mixture has been cooked.
- Serve immediately, or wrap the fritters in aluminum foil and keep in a warm oven until they're all cooked.
- To make the dipping sauce, just mix all the ingredients together in a small bowl.

AVOCADO SALAD

You will need to use ripe avocados for this salad—give them a little squeeze to see if they give a bit. If they are too hard, wait a few days to allow them to ripen before using them. This is a great salad to have with Black Bean, Corn and Feta Tacos on p. 121.

SERVES 4

INGREDIENTS

For the dressing:
· 4 tablespoons extra-virgin olive oil
· 2 tablespoons freshly squeezed lemon or lime juice (from approx. I lemon/lime)
· sea salt and black pepper, to taste

For the salad:
· 2 ripe Hass avocados
· 2 scallions, trimmed and finely chopped
· 2 ripe tomatoes, finely diced
· I fresh red chili (medium heat), seeded and finely chopped, or 6 slices of pickled jalapeños (from a jar), drained (optional)
· 2 tablespoons pine nuts, toasted in a hot frying pan (no oil)
· handful basil leaves, roughly chopped

METHOD

· Make the dressing first. In a cup or small bowl, whisk together the olive oil, lemon or lime juice, a little sea salt and a grind of black pepper. Set this aside.
· Cut the avocados in half, remove the pits, peel, and slice the flesh into a salad bowl, then add the chopped scallions and tomatoes, the chili (or jalapeños), if using, the toasted pine nuts, and chopped fresh basil. Drizzle the dressing over the salad, and toss well. Check the seasoning and add an extra pinch of sea salt and another grind of freshly ground black pepper if you feel it needs more.

SPROUT AND CARROT SALAD

My mum would often rustle up a chef's salad in a huge wooden bowl, making it up as she went along with whatever ingredients were at hand. I still do that today when I can't think of what else to prepare, and there's not much that can't—or doesn't—get thrown in. From the virtuous to the wonderfully sumptuous, there's a salad to go with any occasion. The best bit is you can always remind yourself you're being healthy, and with this one . . . you are.

SERVES 2

INGREDIENTS

· 3 cups alfalfa sprouts, washed and dried
· 2 medium carrots, peeled and grated
· 2 baby gem lettuces or romaine hearts, chopped

For the dressing:
· 2 tablespoons extra-virgin olive oil
· 1 tablespoon balsamic or white wine vinegar
· 1 tablespoon freshly squeezed lemon juice
· pinch sea salt
· freshly ground black pepper, to taste

METHOD

· Combine all the salad ingredients in a medium salad bowl or mixing bowl.
· Drizzle the olive oil, vinegar, and lemon juice over the salad, and toss together well. Season with a pinch of sea salt and some black pepper to taste.

WATERCRESS, RADISH AND FETA SALAD

Salads seem to play a part in pretty much every meal we have during the summer months. I grew up thinking that huge, fresh salads, tossed in a large wooden salad bowl with my mum's home-made dressing, were the norm. Then one day, as a young teenager, I went to my best friend's house for supper and her mum asked if I would like salad. I was amazed when I was served a slice of cucumber, a slice of tomato, and a piece of lettuce with dressing poured over the top! This one goes really well with One-pot Mushroom Rice on p. 126.

SERVES 2

INGREDIENTS

- **3 cups watercress, washed and dried**
- **8 radishes, thinly sliced**
- **¾ cup crumbled feta cheese**

For the dressing:
- **2 tablespoons extra-virgin olive oil**
- **I tablespoon freshly squeezed lemon juice**
- **sea salt and black pepper, to taste**

METHOD

- **First, remove any tough, woody stems from the watercress.**
- **Toss the watercress and radishes in a medium salad bowl and add the feta cheese.**
- **Drizzle the olive oil and lemon juice over the salad and then season with a pinch of sea salt and a couple grinds of black pepper.**
- **Toss together and serve immediately.**

LENTIL AND FETA SALAD

Puy lentils work well in this salad because they have a tender texture and hold their shape when cooked. This salad is a tangy, tasty way of getting lentils into your diet—ensuring a good supply of protein and fiber.

SERVES 2

INGREDIENTS

- 1 cup dried puy lentils
- 2 cups vegetable stock
- 5 scallions, trimmed and finely chopped, or ¼ medium red onion, finely chopped
- 2 medium ripe tomatoes, finely diced
- 3 tablespoons fresh basil or parsley, chopped
- 2 tablespoons freshly squeezed lemon juice (from approx. ½ lemon)
- 2 tablespoons extra-virgin olive oil
- 3 ounces crumbled feta cheese
- pinch sea salt
- black pepper, to taste

METHOD

- Put the lentils into a sieve and rinse them under cold running water, then drain. Transfer them to a medium saucepan and pour the vegetable stock over them. Bring to a boil, reduce heat, and gently simmer for about 15-20 minutes, until the stock has boiled off (or the lentils are al dente).
- Pour the lentils back into the sieve again and give them a quick rinse under running water. Drain well and place them into a medium mixing or salad bowl.
- Stir in the scallions, tomatoes, and basil or parsley. Mix in the lemon juice and olive oil. Add the feta cheese and gently toss it all together. Season with a pinch of sea salt and some freshly ground black pepper, and serve. This salad is best served at room temperature.

HALOUMI AND ROASTED RED PEPPER SALAD

The sweetness of the roasted red peppers alongside the saltiness of the pan-fried haloumi is a vibrant taste combination I really enjoy.

SERVES 2

INGREDIENTS

For the dressing:
· 2 tablespoons extra-virgin olive oil
· I tablespoon red onion or shallot, finely chopped
· I tablespoon freshly squeezed lemon juice (from approx. ½ lemon)

For the salad:
· 2 fresh red peppers (approx. 7 ounces), (or buy a jar of pre-roasted red peppers)
· I pack haloumi cheese (approx. 7-8 ounces)
· 2 tablespoons light olive oil
· I ripe tomato, chopped
· I teaspoon fresh thyme, chopped (optional)
· I teaspoon fresh mint, chopped
· I tablespoon fresh parsley, chopped
· small pinch sea salt
· black pepper, to taste

METHOD

· Make the dressing first: in a cup or small bowl, whisk the extra-virgin olive oil, red onion or shallot, and lemon juice together until combined.
· To roast the red peppers, preheat the broiler to high. Place the whole red peppers on a baking sheet and then under the broiler. Allow the skin to blacken, and then turn the peppers so that eventually the entire surface of each pepper has blackened skin. Turn off the broiler and let the peppers cool slightly. When they have cooled enough for you to handle them, peel away all the skin from the red flesh of the peppers, and discard the skin. Keep the red flesh of the peppers, but discard the stalks and the seeds. Finally, slice the peppers into thin strips.
· Unwrap the haloumi cheese and pat it dry with some paper towels. Cut it into 8 equal slices.
· Cook the haloumi just before you are ready to serve the salad. To do this, heat the oil in a large frying pan over medium heat. When the pan is hot, add the slices of cheese and cook on both sides until lightly browned.
· To assemble the salad, divide the roasted red peppers and tomato evenly and arrange on serving plates. Lay the slices of fried haloumi on top.
· Sprinkle the chopped herbs over the cheese. Drizzle the dressing over the salad and season with a small pinch of sea salt and some freshly ground black pepper.

BALSAMIC ROASTED SHALLOT SALAD

I love shallots: their oniony, garlic flavor goes perfectly with the sweetness of balsamic vinegar when they are baked together, and they are the ideal bite size. This salad looks beautiful too.

SERVES 2

INGREDIENTS

- 6 shallots (approx. 6 ounces), peeled
- I tablespoon balsamic vinegar
- I tablespoon light olive oil
- pinch sea salt
- 6 cherry tomatoes
- 10 walnut halves, broken into pieces
- 2 ½ cups mixed salad greens, e.g. arugula, watercress, baby spinach

For the dressing:
- ½ teaspoon mustard, preferably Dijon
- I teaspoon balsamic vinegar
- I tablespoon extra-virgin olive oil
- small pinch sea salt

METHOD

- Preheat the oven to 350°F.
- Line a baking sheet with aluminum foil and arrange the peeled shallots on top. Drizzle the balsamic vinegar and light olive oil over the shallots, coating the shallots well in the mix. Sprinkle some salt over them.
- Bake the shallots for 30 minutes, checking every 10 minutes or so and tossing them around in their dressing. After 15 minutes, add the cherry tomatoes to the sheet to bake for the remaining 15 minutes. Take the sheet out of the oven and cool to room temperature.
- Meanwhile, in a small, heavy-bottomed frying pan (no need to add oil) toast the walnuts for a couple of minutes over medium heat, shaking often so they don't burn.
- Make the dressing by whisking the mustard, vinegar, and extra-virgin olive oil together in a medium salad bowl. Add a small pinch of sea salt and whisk with a fork. Add the salad greens to the bowl and gently toss the greens so they are lightly coated in dressing.
- Arrange the shallots, tomatoes, and toasted walnuts on top of the dressed salad greens. Ready to serve!

MIXED GREENS, BLUE CHEESE AND RED GRAPE SALAD

This salad makes a great dinner party starter and is really quick to prepare. It never ceases to surprise me just how good blue cheese tastes with red grapes and a simple vinaigrette. One of those odd but brilliant bits of food alchemy!

SERVES 2

INGREDIENTS

- 2 baby gem lettuces or romaine hearts, torn into pieces
- handful mixed greens, such as watercress, baby spinach, and arugula
- 2 ounces blue cheese, such as Maytag or Danish blue, cubed or crumbled
- 8 red grapes, halved
- 10 walnut halves, broken in half and lightly toasted in a frying pan (no oil needed)

For the dressing:
- 4 teaspoons extra-virgin olive oil
- 1 teaspoon freshly squeezed lemon juice
- 1 teaspoon white wine vinegar or similar
- pinch sea salt and black pepper, to taste

METHOD

- Wash and dry the lettuce and mixed greens and place them in a medium salad or mixing bowl, then scatter the blue cheese, red grapes, and walnuts over the top. Drizzle the olive oil, lemon, and white wine vinegar over the salad and toss well. Season with a pinch of sea salt and some freshly ground black pepper and it's ready to serve.

SUPER QUINOA SALAD

Quinoa is a brilliant form of protein and a "superfood," so I am always keen to come up with different recipes that incorporate it. As I love salads and dressings, this is one of my preferred ways of eating quinoa. Served with a piece of toast spread with hummus, it's perfect for lunch.

SERVES 2

INGREDIENTS

- ⅓ cup uncooked quinoa
- 2 scallions, trimmed and finely chopped
- I ripe tomato, finely diced
- I carrot, very thinly sliced lengthwise with a vegetable peeler (see photo!) or finely chopped
- 2 tablespoons fresh parsley, finely chopped

For the dressing:
- I teaspoon Dijon mustard
- juice of I lemon (approx. 2 tablespoons)
- 3 tablespoons extra-virgin olive oil
- pinch sea salt
- black pepper, to taste

METHOD

- Simmer the quinoa in water (approx. ⅔ cup), checking the cooking instructions on the package. Drain and set aside to cool. Then transfer the quinoa, scallions, chopped tomato, sliced carrot, and parsley into a medium salad bowl or mixing bowl. Toss together well.
- In a small bowl or cup, using a fork, whisk the mustard, lemon juice, and olive oil together. Season with a small pinch of salt and some freshly ground black pepper. Drizzle the dressing over the quinoa and vegetables, toss together well, and serve.

NEW POTATO AND ASPARAGUS SALAD WITH MUSTARD DRESSING

This salad works really well served with the Cheesy Quiche on p. 114. But it also makes a great addition to a summer barbecue or picnic. I love to make it when asparagus is in season in the early summer months.

SERVES 2

INGREDIENTS

· I pound new potatoes, washed
· 4 ounces thin asparagus, trimmed

For the dressing:
· 2 tablespoons extra-virgin olive oil
· I tablespoon balsamic vinegar
· 2 teaspoons Dijon mustard (wholegrain or smooth)
· pinch sea salt and freshly ground black pepper, to taste

METHOD

· Place the new potatoes in a large saucepan, cover with water, and bring to a boil over high heat. Then reduce the heat to medium so that the potatoes simmer gently for 12–15 minutes, depending on their size. Test them with a fork to make sure they are definitely cooked through. Then drain them and set aside to cool.
· Simmer the asparagus in boiling water until crisp-tender, about 2–4 minutes, depending on the thickness of the asparagus. Drain, halve crosswise, and cool.
· To make the dressing, mix the olive oil, balsamic vinegar, and Dijon mustard together, and season with a pinch of sea salt and some black pepper.
· Place the new potatoes and asparagus in a medium salad bowl, pour the dressing over them and gently toss together well. Ready to serve.

MAINS

CHEESE AND EGGPLANT OVEN BAKE

This dish is wonderful just as it is, but sometimes I like to vary the recipe for a change. A pinch of chili flakes added to the tomato sauce provides a great kick, and 3 ounces of vegetarian ground meat substitute cooked into the tomato sauce adds substantial "bite" to the meal. Feel free to play around with it too. This is good served with sautéed leeks and a leafy salad or steamed green beans.

SERVES 4

INGREDIENTS

· 4 tablespoons light olive oil
· I medium onion, finely chopped
· 2 cloves garlic, finely chopped
· 14.5 ounce can chopped tomatoes
· I tablespoon tomato paste
· I tablespoon dried mixed herbs, plus a pinch set aside for the olive oil mixture
· sea salt and black pepper, to taste
· I tablespoon soy sauce
· 2 medium eggplants, sliced crosswise into discs ⅓ inch thick
· 3 ounces soft goat cheese or chopped mozzarella
· 4 ounces goat Cheddar or sharp Cheddar, grated
· handful fresh basil leaves (if available), roughly chopped

METHOD

· Preheat the oven to 350°F.
· First make the tomato sauce. In a medium heavy-bottomed saucepan heat 2 tablespoons of the olive oil and gently sauté the chopped onion until softened and slightly golden brown, about 8 minutes. Then stir in the garlic, canned tomatoes, tomato paste, mixed herbs, a small pinch of sea salt, and some black pepper. Simmer gently for 20 minutes, stirring often, until the sauce has thickened. Set aside.
· In a small bowl combine the remaining 2 tablespoons of olive oil, the soy sauce, and the pinch of mixed herbs. Lightly brush both sides of each eggplant slice with the olive oil mixture. Sauté the slices in batches in a large non-stick frying pan over medium heat, cooking for 3–4 minutes on each side, until golden brown.
· Spread a third of the tomato sauce over the bottom of a medium baking dish. Arrange a layer of eggplant slices over the sauce and then spoon I teaspoon of tomato sauce over each eggplant disc. Scatter crumbled pieces of the soft goat cheese over the disc, followed by a layer of eggplant. Spoon the remaining tomato sauce over the eggplant slices and, finally, scatter the basil leaves and grated Cheddar over the top.
· Bake for 15–20 minutes, until the tomato sauce is bubbling and the cheese is lightly brown on top.

MEXICAN BEAN TORTILLA

This recipe has a medley of flavors, colors, and textures—and it makes a bright and satisfying meal in itself.

SERVES 2-4 (I or 2 tortillas per person)

INGREDIENTS

- 2 tablespoons vegetable or light olive oil
- I medium red onion, halved and thinly sliced
- 6 cremini or button mushrooms, thinly sliced
- ½ red pepper, seeded and chopped into bite-sized pieces
- I red chili, seeded and finely chopped, or ½ teaspoon chili flakes (optional—leave out if you do not want the heat)
- I5 ounce can refried beans, or 14.5 ounce can pinto beans, drained
- 4 corn or flour tortillas (approx. 7 inches each in diameter)
- 2 ripe Hass avocados
- 2 limes
- sea salt and freshly ground black pepper, to taste
- 3 cups mixed greens, washed, dried, and roughly chopped
- I tablespoon extra-virgin olive oil, for drizzling over the lettuce leaves
- ¼ cup sour cream or crème fraîche
- 2 tablespoons fresh cilantro, chopped (optional)

METHOD

- Preheat the oven to 350°F (for heating the tortillas).
- In a large frying pan over medium heat, sauté the red onion in the oil for 3 minutes, then add the mushrooms, red pepper, and chili, and sauté for a further 5 minutes, until nearly cooked through.
- Mix in the beans and stir well, until nice and hot, which will take about 5 minutes.
- Prepare the tortillas by wrapping them in aluminum foil and heating for about 10 minutes in the oven, until they're nice and hot.
- Halve the avocados, remove the pits, then scoop out the fruit with a spoon and cut it into bite-sized cubes. Put them into a medium mixing bowl. Squeeze the juice of I ½ limes over the avocado, and sprinkle a pinch of sea salt over, then mix well.
- In a separate salad bowl, toss the greens with a drizzle (I tablespoon) of olive oil and the juice of half the remaining lime. Season with sea salt and black pepper.
- To assemble: put a warm tortilla on each serving plate. Spoon the bean mix onto each one and spread it across the base of each tortilla, about ¾ inch thick. Top with the salad, and then the diced avocado. Dollop a spoonful of sour cream on top and follow with a grind of freshly ground black pepper. Garnish with some chopped cilantro (if you like it). Eat immediately!

CHEESY QUICHE

This is my version of one of my mum's recipes that I love to pass on to friends and family—it's a sharing recipe! The secret to making the quiche puff up and rise, is to cook it at a high temperature. I like to serve it with crushed buttered new potatoes and steamed vegetables, or a leafy green salad. Leftover quiche can be kept in the fridge for a few days, so it's great warmed up for lunches or sliced and wrapped up for picnics.

SERVES 6

INGREDIENTS

· 10 ounces Shortcrust Pie Pastry, homemade (see p. 166) or 1 pre-made refrigerated pie crust
· flour, for dusting work surface
· 2 tablespoons vegetable or light olive oil
· 6 medium onions, finely chopped (I like to use 3 red onions and 3 white onions)
· 1 tablespoon mixed fresh herbs (such as parsley, thyme, etc.), chopped
· 6 large, free-range eggs
· 2 cups milk
· 8 ounces sharp Cheddar cheese, grated
· freshly ground black pepper, to taste

METHOD

· Preheat the oven to 350°F.
· Roll out the pastry on a clean, lightly floured surface to about a 12 inch diameter, $\frac{1}{8}$ inch thick, and then line a metal pie pan (9-10 inches) with the pastry. To keep the crust from becoming too soggy once the filling is poured in, you will need to pre-bake (blind bake) the pastry. To do this, line the pastry in the pie dish with parchment paper and then fill it with just enough dried beans or rice to cover the bottom. Bake for 10 minutes. Allow the beans or rice to cool, then carefully remove them and the parchment paper and set aside (the beans or rice can be stored in a container to reuse for blind baking in the future). Put the pie dish back in the oven to bake for 5 minutes more. Remove the crust and set aside.
· Now turn up the oven to 400°F.
· In a medium frying pan over medium heat, sauté the onions in the oil for 10–15 minutes, until they soften and turn golden, then mix in the herbs. Take it off the heat and let them cool slightly.
· In a large mixing bowl, beat the eggs and whisk in the milk, so that the eggs are light and have air bubbles. Stir in the grated cheese and fried onions, and season with black pepper.
· Pour the mixture into the pastry shell and bake for 30–35 minutes, until the filling has risen and is well browned on top. The center should have a spring to the touch when you press it gently in the middle.

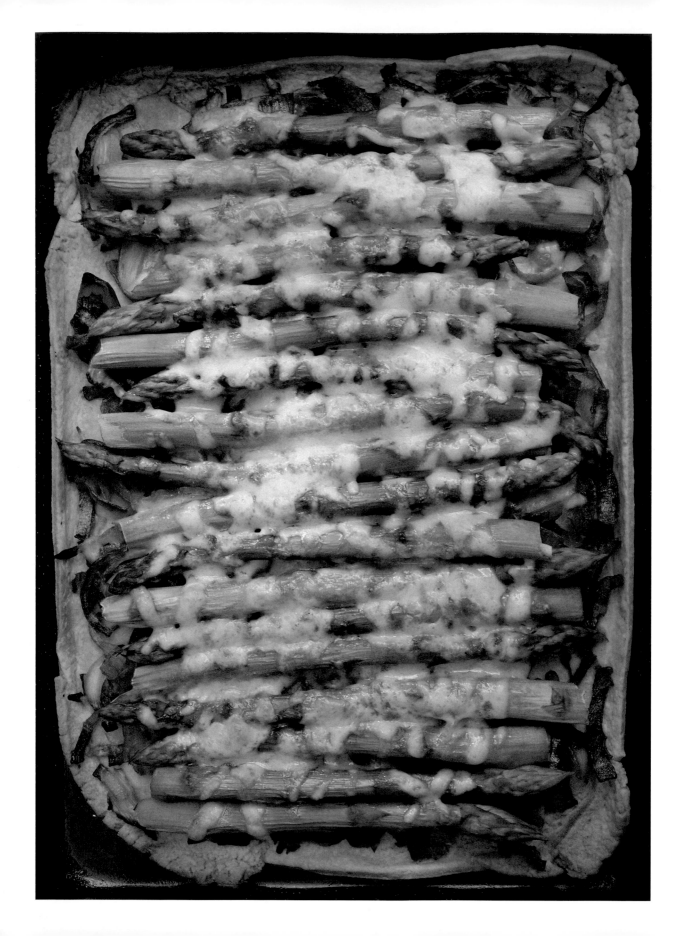

ASPARAGUS SUMMER TART

The slow-cooked, sweet red onions add an extra dimension to this asparagus tart. Making it for friends is great because you can prepare it before your guests arrive and then pop it in the oven 15 minutes before you are ready to eat. I like to serve this with a simple green salad with a lemon and olive oil dressing.

SERVES 4

INGREDIENTS

- 8 ounces Cream Cheese Pastry (see p. 164) or 1 store-bought refrigerated pie crust
- 2 tablespoons vegetable or light olive oil
- 4 medium red onions, thinly sliced
- large bunch fresh asparagus (approx. 1 pound)
- 5 ounces good melting cheese, such as Gruyère, Taleggio, smoked Cheddar or goat Cheddar, cubed or grated
- freshly ground black pepper, to taste

METHOD

- Preheat the oven to 325°F.
- Roll out the pastry to about ⅛ inch thick and lay it on a baking sheet (approx. 12 x 8 inches) to fit the edges. To blind bake the pastry crust, lay parchment paper onto the rolled pastry, and then spread baking beans or rice on top to gently weight it down. Bake it for 10 minutes, then remove the paper and beans and bake again for about 5 minutes, until the pastry is lightly golden but not fully cooked.
- For the filling: heat the oil in a medium heavy-bottomed frying pan over medium/low heat and gently fry the onions until they are soft and caramelized (about 15 minutes).
- To prepare the asparagus, clean all the spears under cold water and then snap or cut off just the woody ends (you can discard these). Boil in just enough water to cover them, for 2–3 minutes, depending on thickness. They should be slightly undercooked, as they will finish cooking in the oven.
- Spread the caramelized onions evenly over the pre-baked pastry crust and then arrange the asparagus over the onions. Sprinkle the cheese over the top and season with freshly ground black pepper.
- Bake the tart in the oven for about 15 minutes, or until the pastry is golden and the cheese is bubbling hot and turning golden brown. Cut into portions, and serve.

WHITE BEAN GRAVY STEW

This stew has a luxurious rich gravy and goes well with steamed long-grain rice, or over mashed potatoes with some steamed seasonal vegetables, and Cauliflower Cheese (p. 141) on the side. As a variation, I sometimes like to add a glug (about ½ cup) of red wine just before adding the stock, and then I let it simmer gently for 5 minutes to allow the alcohol to burn off. A pinch of red chili flakes adds a nice hot kick if you're in the mood.

The veggie burger needs to be a firm one that's made from soy protein, not soft potato or vegetables, otherwise it won't hold its shape when cooking.

SERVES 2

INGREDIENTS

· 2 tablespoons vegetable or light olive oil
· 2 medium leeks (approx. 7 ounces), trimmed, washed, and chopped—or 2 medium onions, chopped
· 8 cremini or button mushrooms, thinly sliced
· I tablespoon soy sauce
· 15 ounce can white beans (such as cannellini), drained
· I veggie burger, cooked and chopped into cubes (optional)
· I tablespoon chopped fresh parsley, or 2 teaspoons dried mixed herbs
· 1½ tablespoons cornstarch
· 1¼ cups vegetable stock
· sea salt and black pepper, to taste
· pinch red chili flakes (optional)

METHOD

· In a large saucepan or a large frying pan with deep sides, heat the oil over medium heat and gently sauté the leeks or onions for 5–8 minutes, until they are soft and starting to turn golden. Stir in the mushrooms and soy sauce, and fry for 5 minutes more. Add the chili (if using). Stir in the beans, the cubed veggie burger, and herbs, and allow them to heat through for a couple of minutes.
· Mix the cornstarch and vegetable stock together and pour it into the stew, stirring continuously to make sure it doesn't get lumpy. Simmer gently for 10 minutes, stirring often, until the mixture has thickened to a creamy consistency. Check the seasoning and add a little salt and pepper if needed.
· And now it's ready to serve. It's good with a spoonful of crème fraîche or sour cream and freshly ground black pepper on top.

SPINACH, LEEK AND ZUCCHINI FRITTATA

This makes a quick and nutritious meal. I sometimes have it for brunch too, but then I would leave out the zucchini. It's great served with potato salad or cooked new potatoes tossed in butter and herbs.

SERVES 2

INGREDIENTS

- 7 ounces fresh spinach
- 2 tablespoons vegetable or light olive oil
- I leek, trimmed, washed, and finely chopped
- I medium onion, finely chopped
- I medium zucchini, trimmed and cut into small cubes
- I teaspoon chopped fresh oregano, or I teaspoon dried herbs
- I teaspoon chopped fresh or dried thyme
- 5 large, free-range eggs
- I tablespoon butter, for frying
- 3 ounces feta cheese
- sea salt and freshly ground black pepper, to taste

METHOD

- Wash the fresh spinach leaves thoroughly and then cook them in a medium saucepan over medium heat until wilted. The spinach releases a lot of liquid when cooking, so you don't need to add any water. Once the leaves have wilted, remove them from the heat and cool slightly. When you can handle the spinach, squeeze out the excess liquid, and chop up the leaves. Set aside.
- Now heat the oil in a medium frying pan over medium heat. Add the leeks, onions, zucchini, and herbs and sauté them for about 8 minutes (so that you can hear the sizzling) until they are turning golden. Add the cooked spinach, tossing to combine and then transfer the vegetables to a dish or plate while you prepare the eggs.
- Preheat the broiler to high. Crack the eggs into a mixing bowl and beat them together.
- Melt the butter in a medium frying pan over medium-high heat. Pour in the eggs. Scatter the cooked vegetables over the eggs and crumble the feta cheese evenly over the top. Add some freshly ground black pepper and a pinch of salt. Cook for a couple of minutes, until the eggs are turning golden around the edges of the pan.
- Place the pan under the broiler, keeping the handle turned away, so that it does not overheat. Cook until the eggs are set on top.
- Gently slide the frittata onto a serving plate and cut into pieces. I like this served warm, but it can be eaten at room temperature, too.

BLACK BEAN, SWEET CORN AND FETA TACOS

I've always loved tacos but this is a little deviation from how I usually make them, to include the corn. My mum loved Mexican food and she also loved corn, eating it from the cob when it was in season. I think it adds a lovely, crunchy texture to this particular taco combination. The added bonus is that these are quick and easy to make.

SERVES 2 (2 tacos per person)

INGREDIENTS

· 3 tablespoons vegetable or light olive oil
· I medium onion, finely chopped
· 15 ounce can black beans
· 3 cloves garlic, finely chopped
· 4 slices pickled jalapeño (from a jar), chopped, or ½ teaspoon chili flakes, or ½ teaspoon finely chopped fresh red chili
· pinch sea salt, or to taste
· ½ teaspoon ground cumin
· 3 ounces sweet corn, cut (I large cob fresh, or frozen, or canned)
· 4 taco shells
· 3 ounces feta cheese, crumbled
· juice of I lime

METHOD

· Preheat the oven to 350°F.
· Heat the oil in a medium frying pan over medium heat and sauté the chopped onion for 5 minutes. Drain and rinse the black beans in a sieve, and then stir them into the onion in the pan. Add the garlic, jalapeño or chili, the sea salt, and the cumin, and heat for 5 minutes until cooked through.
· To cook the corn (if fresh), place it in a small saucepan with boiling water and simmer for a couple of minutes until hot; drain.
· In the meantime, wrap the taco shells in aluminum foil and put them in the oven for 5–10 minutes to heat up.
· When the taco shells are warm, remove them from the oven, then divide the bean mix evenly between the 4 tacos, top with the cooked corn and, finally, sprinkle the crumbled feta over the top. Finish off with a little squeeze of lime juice, and serve hot.

BUTTERED ZUCCHINI AND CHEESY POLENTA

Polenta is basically Italian grits . . . it can be a delicious alternative to mashed potatoes because it has a great, unctuous consistency and can be flavored for a more intense taste. This way of cooking it gives it a savory edge, which acts as a base for the subtle zucchini topping. You could substitute mushrooms for the zucchini, or toss in a handful of sliced mushrooms to cook along with them.

SERVES 4

INGREDIENTS

For the buttered zucchini:
- 2 tablespoons butter
- 3 medium zucchini, trimmed and cut into long thin strips approx. ¼ inch thick
- 2 cloves garlic, finely chopped
- 2 tablespoons fresh parsley, chopped
- sea salt and black pepper, to taste
- squeeze of lemon juice (½ lemon)

For the polenta:
- 2½ cups vegetable stock
- 2½ cups milk
- 2 cups quick-cook polenta
- 7 tablespoons butter
- ½ cup grated Parmesan cheese or sharp Cheddar

METHOD

- Heat the butter in a medium frying pan over medium-low heat and add the zucchini, stirring until well coated in the butter. Stir in the garlic and parsley and sauté for 5–8 minutes, or until the zucchini are tender. Season with sea salt and pepper, and then squeeze a little lemon juice over the zucchini and combine well.
- In a large saucepan, heat the stock and milk together until almost boiling, then gradually whisk in the polenta. Keep stirring until the mixture has thickened, although you still want it to be soft and pourable. Add a little more milk or water, if necessary. Stir in the butter and cheese and season with black pepper.
- Spoon the polenta onto plates and arrange the buttered zucchini on top. Serve hot.

LEEK AND PEA RISOTTO

This silky, creamy risotto looks so good with the subtle green of the leeks and peas, and it has a wonderfully smooth texture. You can play around with the vegetables you use, for instance, substituting 6 shallots for the leeks.

SERVES 4

INGREDIENTS

- 3 tablespoons light olive oil
- I tablespoon butter
- 2 medium leeks, finely chopped
- I medium onion, finely chopped
- I stalk celery, finely chopped
- 1¼ cups risotto rice
- 2 cloves garlic, finely chopped
- 2 teaspoons fresh thyme or parsley, chopped
- ⅔ cup dry white wine (optional)
- I quart hot vegetable stock, plus more stock or boiled water, if needed
- 1⅓ cups frozen or fresh shelled peas, or chopped green beans
- sea salt and black pepper, to taste
- ¼ cup grated Parmesan cheese , plus more for serving

METHOD

- Melt the oil and butter together in a large heavy-bottomed saucepan over medium heat. Stir in the chopped leeks, onion and celery and then sauté gently for about I5 minutes, to allow the leeks and onions to sweat and become translucent, but not brown. Add the rice and garlic and mix well, coating the rice in the oil, and cook, stirring often, for a couple of minutes, to allow the rice to heat through, but not brown. Now stir in the herbs and the white wine (if using).
- Add a couple ladlefuls of the hot stock (about ¾ cup), enough to cover the rice. Stir well, and simmer gently, stirring frequently, until the stock is nearly absorbed, but do not let the rice cook too quickly. Gradually add more stock and keep stirring, until all of it has been absorbed; do not allow the risotto to dry out, you want a thick, soupy consistency. Stir in the peas halfway through cooking the rice, after about 7 minutes. After about I5 minutes the rice should be cooked through but still al dente. If you run out of stock and the rice is not cooked yet, then use some extra stock or hot water to finish off—but be careful not to let it overcook and become soggy or sticky.
- Season with black pepper; taste the rice and add salt, if needed. Remove from the heat and stir in the Parmesan cheese. Mix well and let stand for I or 2 minutes. Then serve immediately, with extra Parmesan cheese and black pepper sprinkled over the top.

ONE-POT MUSHROOM RICE

Taking the time to slow-cook the onions and mushrooms before adding the rice gives it much more flavor. Plus, it doesn't create a lot of dirty dishes to wash! My best friend from school says that she can't get her son to eat mushrooms except for this dish that he requests specifically.

SERVES 4

INGREDIENTS

· **3 tablespoons light olive oil**
· **3 medium red onions, finely chopped**
· **7 ounces button, cremini, or small portobello mushrooms, finely chopped**
· **2 teaspoons fresh or dried mixed herbs**
· **I tablespoon soy sauce**
· **I cup long-grain rice**
· **2 cups vegetable stock**
· **¼ cup frozen peas**
· **sea salt and black pepper, to taste**
· **grated Parmesan cheese, sharp Cheddar, or crème fraîche, to serve (optional)**

METHOD

· Heat the olive oil in a large saucepan over medium heat, stir in the onions and sauté them for 8 minutes. Next, stir in the mushrooms, mixed herbs, and soy sauce, and gently sauté them for 10–12 minutes more, until the natural juices from the mushrooms have evaporated and they have started to turn golden brown.
· Add the rice and stir well for a minute until well coated. Pour in the vegetable stock and simmer gently for about 15 minutes, or until the rice has cooked through but has not had a chance to turn too soft.
· Stir in the frozen peas and heat through; season with sea salt and black pepper. Serve topped with grated cheese or a spoonful of crème fraîche, if you like.

SAGE AND ONION "ROAST"

This is the baked terrine I like to make for Sunday lunch, served with all the traditional trimmings of roast vegetables, steamed greens, and Yorkshire puddings. Leftovers can be reheated and served midweek with gravy, steamed green beans, and a generous spoonful of horseradish on the side.

SERVES 4

INGREDIENTS

- 3 tablespoons light olive oil
- 2 medium onions, finely chopped
- 2 stalks celery, finely chopped
- 1/3 cup pine nuts, lightly toasted in a frying pan (no oil needed)
- 1/3 cup walnut halves, chopped
- 3/4 cup chestnuts, peeled, cooked, and chopped
- 3 tablespoons fresh sage, chopped
- 3 veggie burgers, cooked and crumbled
- 1 1/4 cups dried breadcrumbs
- 3/4 cup vegetable stock
- 3 large, free-range eggs, beaten
- sea salt and black pepper, to taste

METHOD

- Preheat the oven to 375°F. Line a 9 inch loaf pan (about 4 inches deep) with parchment paper.
- In a large frying pan over medium heat, heat the olive oil and gently sauté the chopped onions and celery for about 5–10 minutes. Stir in the pine nuts, walnuts, chestnuts, chopped sage, and the crumbled veggie burgers. Sauté for a minute or two until heated through. Now add the breadcrumbs and cook for another 8–10 minutes.
- Stir in the vegetable stock and cook for a couple of minutes. Transfer the mixture to a large mixing bowl and let cool for a couple of minutes. Then stir in the beaten eggs, season with salt and plenty of black pepper, and mix together well.
- Spoon the mixture into the lined loaf pan and press it down evenly.
- Bake the terrine in the middle of the oven for 30 minutes. Remove it from the oven and turn it upside down onto a non-stick baking sheet, peeling away the parchment. Put it back in the oven to bake for 30 more minutes, until the outside is crisp and golden. Slice and serve with Red Onion Gravy (see p. 171).

WINTER WARMER HOTPOT

I make this a lot, because it is packed with fresh vegetables and easy to put together—by allowing it to slow-cook in the oven it comes out full of flavor. I like it served with a dollop of crème fraîche or sour cream on top and some freshly ground black pepper. A meal-in-one-dish.

SERVES 4

INGREDIENTS

- 3 large potatoes (or 6 medium), cut crosswise into thin round slices approx. ¼ inch thick
- 3 medium onions, halved then cut crosswise into thin slices
- 2 medium carrots, cut into cubes
- 8 ounces green beans, trimmed and chopped
- 15 ounce can white beans (such as cannellini), drained
- 3 vegetarian sausages (or burgers), cooked and chopped into chunky bite-sized pieces (optional)
- 2 tablespoons chopped fresh parsley, or 2 teaspoons dried mixed herbs
- 3 ⅓ cups vegetable stock, mixed with 1 tablespoon cornstarch
- 2 tablespoons light olive oil, for drizzling on top
- black pepper, to taste
- butter or olive oil for finishing

METHOD

- Preheat the oven to 350°F.
- Arrange half of the potato slices in the bottom of a casserole or baking dish (about 11 inches). Layer all of the onion slices over them, then scatter the carrots and green beans over the onion, followed by the beans and then the sausage or burger pieces (if using). Sprinkle in the herbs and finish with a final layer of the remaining potato slices.
- Now carefully pour in the vegetable stock, which should come to about ⅓ inch below the final (top) layer of potato. Drizzle olive oil over the top, grind some black pepper over it, and cover the dish with aluminum foil.
- Place the dish on the middle rack in the oven. Cook for 1 hour, 45 minutes, then take off the foil, dot the potatoes with butter or olive oil, and cook for 15 minutes more, until the top layer of potatoes is golden and slightly crisp.

SHEPHERD'S PIE

This is classic comfort food because it has the indulgence of a creamy mashed potato topping that goes perfectly with juicy gravy. I like it with a squeeze of ketchup on the side! It's also versatile—you can swap the frozen peas for green beans, you can play around with the herbs, and a splash of red wine in the gravy is usually a welcome extra. If you have any left over, this is such a good dish to reheat on demand throughout the week. I like this served with lightly buttered spinach.

SERVES 6

INGREDIENTS

For the topping:
- 2 pounds potatoes (such as russet), peeled and chopped into large cubes
- 4 tablespoons butter
- ⅔ cup milk
- I teaspoon mustard, preferably Dijon (smooth or wholegrain)
- pinch sea salt and black pepper, to taste
- 3 ounces sharp Cheddar, grated (optional)

For the filling:
- 2 tablespoons vegetable or light olive oil
- I large onion, finely chopped
- I garlic clove, finely chopped
- I stalk celery, trimmed and finely chopped
- I medium carrot, finely chopped
- 8 ounces green beans, chopped, or I cup frozen peas
- 6 cremini or button mushrooms, chopped into small pieces
- 7 ounces vegetarian ground meat substitute
- 2 tablespoons cornstarch
- 3 cups vegetable stock
- 2 tablespoons tamari or soy sauce
- I tablespoon tomato paste
- I tablespoon chopped herbs (fresh parsley and oregano if possible), or I teaspoon dried mixed herbs
- ½ cup red wine (optional)

METHOD

- Preheat the oven to 350°F.
- Place the potato chunks into a large saucepan, cover with water, and bring to a boil. Boil for 15–20 minutes, until they are tender, then drain.
- Mash the potatoes well and return the pan to low heat. Stir in the butter, milk, and mustard and whisk with a fork to make a light, fluffy, and smooth mash. Season with a pinch of sea salt and black pepper.
- To make the filling, heat the oil in a large heavy-bottomed pan over medium heat, and gently fry the onion for 5 minutes. Stir in the garlic, celery, carrot, green beans, mushrooms, and finally the meat substitute, mix well and cook for 2–3 minutes more.
- Put the cornstarch into a measuring cup and slowly whisk in the vegetable stock. Pour this over the vegetables, stirring well, and increase the heat to bring it to a gentle simmer. Add the tamari or soy sauce, the tomato, paste, and herbs (and also the red wine, if using). Let it gently simmer for 15–20 minutes.
- Transfer the filling into a large ovenproof dish. Top with large spoonfuls of the mashed potato, gently smoothing it over with a fork so the potato covers the filling. Sprinkle the grated cheese over the top with a little more black pepper.
- Bake in the oven for 30 minutes until the top is golden brown and the filling is bubbling.

WHITE SPAGHETTI SAUCE

This is a fast and simple pasta sauce. It is very tasty and quite indulgent. But it is white! And I have an obsessive need to have something green on my plate to make a meal feel complete. With that in mind, I love this served with a watercress or arugula salad, or steamed green vegetables such as spinach or green beans.

SERVES 4

INGREDIENTS

- 1 tablespoon light olive oil
- 1 cup crème fraîche
- 2 tablespoons milk
- generous grinding fresh black pepper, or to taste
- 12 ounces dried spaghetti or linguine (or other dried pasta of your choice)
- 3 ounces grated Parmesan cheese, plus more to serve
- pinch sea salt, or to taste

METHOD

- Gently heat the oil in a large frying pan over low heat. Add the crème fraîche and milk, and stir well until heated through. Grind in some black pepper, remove from the heat, and set it aside.
- Now cook the pasta in a large, heavy-bottomed saucepan of boiling, salted water (check the package for cooking time—about 8–10 minutes and the pasta should be cooked but still firm to the bite, not soggy).
- Once the pasta is cooked, drain it in a colander, then add it to the white sauce in the frying pan and mix together until the pasta is coated in the sauce, heating it through again over medium-low heat. Stir in the grated Parmesan and serve hot with extra Parmesan cheese, some more ground black pepper, and a pinch of sea salt on top, according to your taste. Best eaten immediately.

MAC & CHEESE WITH CRISPY TOPPING

I love macaroni and cheese with a blob of tomato ketchup on the side and served with nothing more than some cooked frozen peas. It's so satisfying when you've had a busy day and are in need of proper comfort food.

SERVES 4

INGREDIENTS

· 14 ounces dried macaroni
· 2 tablespoons butter
· ¼ cup all-purpose flour
· 2 cups milk
· 1 teaspoon Dijon mustard
· 7 ounces sharp Cheddar cheese, grated
· ½ cup grated Parmesan cheese (or similar)
· black pepper, to taste

For the crispy topping:
· ½ cup dried breadcrumbs
· 3 tablespoons Parmesan cheese, finely grated
· 1 tablespoon fresh parsley, finely chopped
· 1 tablespoon mixed pumpkin and sesame seeds, finely chopped (optional)

METHOD

· Cook the macaroni in a large pan of boiling, salted water. Stir it from time to time to make sure the pasta doesn't stick together or to the bottom of the pan. Undercook the pasta by a couple of minutes (check the package for cooking time and deduct 2 minutes), so it is not quite cooked through, as it will go in the oven to finish later. Drain the pasta in a colander and set it aside while you make the topping.
· Preheat the oven to 375°F.
· Make the topping by mixing together the breadcrumbs, Parmesan cheese, fresh parsley, and finely chopped seeds in a medium bowl.
· To make the cheese sauce, melt the butter in a large, heavy-bottomed saucepan over medium-low heat and then stir in the flour, mixing very well for about 20 seconds to make a paste. Gradually add the milk, stirring constantly, until thick and creamy. Stir in the mustard. Take the sauce off the heat and then stir in the grated cheese, mixing well, until it is melted and the sauce is completely smooth—if it seems too thick, add a little more milk. Season with black pepper.
· Add the cooked pasta to the pan and mix the pasta and sauce together so it is all coated.
· Transfer the macaroni to a baking dish, spreading it out evenly. Sprinkle the breadcrumb mix over the top, then bake for 20–25 minutes, until the sauce is bubbling and the topping has turned golden and crisp.

MUSHROOM AND LEEK LASAGNA

This is a good dinner party dish that can be assembled in advance and then put in the oven, when your guests have arrived, to cook for 40 minutes or so before serving.

SERVES 4–6

INGREDIENTS

· 1½ ounces dried porcini mushrooms
· 2 tablespoons vegetable or light olive oil
· 3 medium leeks, trimmed, washed, and finely chopped
· 1 medium onion, finely chopped
· 9 ounces cremini or button mushrooms, thinly sliced
· 2 teaspoons fresh thyme, chopped
· 2 large, free-range eggs
· 7 ounces feta cheese, crumbled
· 9 ounces cooked lasagna noodles (12 to 15)
· 3 ounces soft goat cheese or cream cheese
· 7 ounces sharp Cheddar or goat Cheddar, grated
· freshly ground black pepper, to taste

For the sauce:
· 2 tablespoons vegetable or light olive oil
· 3 tablespoons all-purpose or light spelt flour
· ¾ cup porcini stock (reserved from soaking the dried mushrooms, see method)
· 2 cups milk
· sea salt and black pepper, to taste

METHOD

· Preheat the oven to 350°F.
· Rehydrate the dried porcini mushrooms in a bowl of warm water (about 15 minutes), or as per the package instructions.
· Meanwhile, in a large frying pan heat the 2 tablespoons of oil over medium heat, add the chopped leeks and onion and sauté for 6–8 minutes, until they are soft and golden. Then stir in the sliced mushrooms and sauté until tender, about 5 minutes more.
· Once the porcini mushrooms are rehydrated, reserve ¾ cup of the stock to make the sauce, then drain the mushrooms. Mix them, along with the thyme, into the vegetables in the pan. Sauté for 5–10 minutes, until cooked through. Season with salt and black pepper, and set aside.
· To make the porcini sauce, gently heat the oil in a medium saucepan over medium-low heat, then stir in the flour and stir together. Gradually add the reserved porcini stock and stir well to avoid lumps. Slowly add the milk, stirring constantly, and then simmer very gently, stirring often, until the sauce has thickened to a creamy consistency that coats the spoon. Season with a pinch of sea salt and some freshly ground black pepper. Take the sauce off the heat and set it aside.
· Now for the final component. In a small mixing bowl, beat the 2 eggs and mix in the crumbled feta cheese.

· To assemble the lasagna, spread a third of the sauce in the bottom of a medium baking dish (about 10 inches). Cover this evenly with a layer of the lasagna noodles, and spread a third of the mushroom and leek mix over the pasta. Now spread all of the egg and feta mix evenly over this, followed by another layer of lasagna noodles. Top with another third of the porcini sauce and then a third of the mushroom and leek mix. Crumble the goat cheese (or cream cheese) over the mushroom and leek mix and lay another layer of lasagna noodles on top. Pour the remaining sauce over the pasta and add the remaining mushroom and leek mix, and finally sprinkle the grated Cheddar evenly over the top.

· Grind some black pepper over the lasagna and then put it into the oven for 30–40 minutes, until it is golden and bubbling hot. (If the lasagna is pre-assembled and refrigerated, allow an extra 5–10 minutes to heat through.)

· Remove from the oven and serve. This lasagna is great eaten with a fresh chopped salad or seasonal steamed vegetables.

CAULIFLOWER CHEESE

Cauliflower cheese is an old classic and a firm favorite. It's a good way of getting kids to eat their veggies, too—I sometimes add broccoli or a handful of frozen peas, or serve it with baked beans. My preference is always for sharp Cheddar, since it adds real punch, and I sometimes like to use whole wheat flour to give the sauce a bit of extra texture.

SERVES 2 as a main course, or 4 as a side dish

INGREDIENTS

- 1 medium head cauliflower, approx. 1⅓ pounds
- 2 tablespoons vegetable or light olive oil or butter
- 3 tablespoons all-purpose or light spelt flour
- 2 cups milk
- 1 teaspoon Dijon mustard
- 7 ounces sharp Cheddar, grated
- ½ cup Parmesan cheese, grated
- black pepper, to taste

METHOD

- Remove the outer leaves of the cauliflower and discard, then cut the cauliflower into quarters. Place the 4 pieces into a steamer basket and steam the cauliflower for 10 minutes, or until it is just tender (it will continue to cook in the oven). Arrange the cauliflower pieces in a medium baking dish and set it aside.
- Preheat the oven to 350°F.
- In the meantime you can start on the sauce. In a medium saucepan gently heat the oil or butter over medium-low heat. Stir in the flour for about 30 seconds, then add a fifth of the milk. Stir well until it thickens, then add another fifth of the milk and stir again until it is thickened—and continue in this way until all the milk is used up. Add the mustard and stir it in well. Now take the sauce off the heat and add most of the cheese, holding back 1 tablespoon of the Cheddar and 1 tablespoon of the Parmesan cheese, which you will use to sprinkle on top before you put the dish in the oven. Mix well until the cheese is completely melted. Add a few grinds of black pepper.
- Pour the cheese sauce over the cauliflower pieces in the baking dish. Sprinkle the remaining grated cheese over the top.
- Put in the oven and bake for 12–15 minutes, until the top is golden brown and the sauce is bubbling hot.

YUMMY SPICY RICE NOODLES

This noodle dish is totally addictive. It's spicy, peanutty, and irresistible for either lunch or dinner. If I have friends over for dinner, I like to serve Corn Fritters (see p. 82) as a starter, and then Coconut Rice Pudding with Chocolate Sauce (see p. 206) for dessert. The main thing is to not to overcook the rice noodles since they will get heated again when you warm all the ingredients together at the end.

SERVES 4–6

INGREDIENTS

For the sauce:
- 3 tablespoons crunchy peanut butter
- 2 tablespoons chili pepper jam, or ¼ cup sweet chili sauce
- 1¼ cups hot vegetable stock
- 1 tablespoon toasted sesame oil
- 2 tablespoons soy or tamari sauce
- 6 tablespoons coconut milk

For the noodles and vegetables:
- 3 bundles flat rice noodles (approx. 14 ounces)
- 2 tablespoons toasted sesame oil, plus more for the noodles
- 1 ounce whole baby corn, cut into pieces, or 1 cup canned or frozen corn kernels
- 2 medium carrots, thinly sliced
- 1 medium red onion, halved and thinly sliced
- 4 ounces green beans, chopped
- 5 ounces broccoli, broken into small florets
- 3 cloves garlic, finely chopped
- chopped peanuts and cilantro, to serve (optional)

METHOD

- Put all of the sauce ingredients into a mixing bowl, and mix together well, so that the heated vegetable stock softens the ingredients. Set aside while you prepare the vegetables.
- Cook the rice noodles following the package instructions (but maybe a minute less than suggested), then drain the noodles in a colander and toss them in a little sesame oil to keep them from sticking together. You do not want the noodles too soft, but still al dente, since they will be heated again in the vegetables and sauce at the end.
- To prepare the vegetables, heat the 2 tablespoons of sesame oil in a large frying pan with deep sides over medium-high heat (or use a wok or big saucepan). Stir-fry all the vegetables together with the garlic for about 3 minutes, until they are just starting to soften slightly.
- Pour the sauce onto the vegetables in the pan and simmer gently for 4–5 minutes, until the vegetables are cooked through but still have a good bite to them and are not too soft.
- Now stir in the cooked rice noodles. Toss together well and heat through. I serve this hot, and sometimes garnish the dish with chopped peanuts and chopped cilantro.

ZUCCHINI AND LEMON SPAGHETTI

This recipe came about when I was scanning the contents of my kitchen cupboards and fridge, trying to find something I could whip up in less than half an hour that wouldn't create lots of dish-washing chaos. I like the sharpness of the feta combined with the freshness of the zucchini and the tanginess of the lemon. Also the flecks of herbs add an extra dimension that makes this dish burst with flavor.

SERVES 2

INGREDIENTS

- 7 ounces dried spaghetti
- 3 tablespoons light olive oil, plus more for drizzling
- 2 medium zucchini, thinly sliced lengthwise
- 3 cloves garlic, finely chopped
- 1½ teaspoons fresh sage, chopped
- 1½ teaspoons fresh rosemary, chopped
- 2 tablespoons grated Parmesan cheese or Pecorino Romano cheese, plus more for serving (optional)
- 4 ounces feta cheese, crumbled (optional)
- zest of ½ lemon
- sea salt and black pepper, to taste

METHOD

- First cook the spaghetti (check the package for specific instructions) by bringing a large saucepan of water to a boil, adding a couple of large pinches of sea salt and then the spaghetti; it should take about 8–10 minutes to cook. Stir every so often so the strands of pasta don't stick together. When the pasta is just cooked (al dente), drain it in a colander, drizzle with a little olive oil and then mix to lightly coat the pasta and prevent the strands from sticking together. Set it aside.
- You can use the same saucepan to make the sauce. Pour in the 3 tablespoons of olive oil and heat over medium heat, then add the zucchini and sauté for 4–5 minutes, before adding the garlic and herbs and mixing well. Sauté for a couple more minutes, to allow all the flavors to come together and the zucchini to cook through.
- Return the cooked spaghetti to the pan and heat through, then mix in the cheese and lemon zest, and season with a little sea salt (you may not need much since the feta cheese is salty) and a good grind of black pepper. Serve, with a little more grated cheese sprinkled over, if you wish.

TOMATO AND RED WINE SAUCE

This is a really versatile sauce that can form the base for so many pasta dishes. You can add 3 ounces of soy or vegetable ground "meat" to make it into an alternative Bolognese sauce. My eldest son likes to add a chopped red pepper when he is frying the onions as a variation, too. Once you get the basic sauce right, you'll find your own variations.

SERVES 6

INGREDIENTS

· 3 tablespoons light olive oil
· 2 medium onions, finely chopped
· 4 cloves garlic, finely chopped
· 28 ounce can chopped tomatoes
· 2 tablespoons tomato paste
· good glug of red wine (approx. 1/3 cup)
· I tablespoon dried mixed herbs, or I tablespoon chopped fresh oregano
· small handful fresh basil, if available, plus more to serve
· freshly grated Parmesan cheese, to serve

METHOD

· Heat the olive oil over medium heat in a large deep-sided frying pan, and then add the chopped onions—you want to hear a nice sizzle as they cook. Gently sauté them for about 10 minutes, until they are caramelized, and then add the chopped garlic. Give it a good stir with a wooden spoon to make sure the garlic is well coated in olive oil, and cook for another minute.
· Add the chopped tomatoes and stir well, then mix in the tomato paste. Gently simmer for about 5 minutes. Then, as the sauce simmers, stir in the red wine and dried mixed herbs or fresh oregano.
· Gently cook for another 15 minutes. Tear up the basil and add that to the sauce too.
· Serve topped with a fresh basil leaf and some grated Parmesan.

BASICS
AND
SIDES

ROASTED ROSEMARY NEW POTATOES

If you do not have new potatoes, then other roasting potatoes can be used instead—just chop them into chunks and parboil, and follow the recipe in the same way. These are lovely served with White Bean Gravy Stew (p. 118), or with Sage and Onion "Roast" (p. 130) and Red Onion Gravy (p. 171), with some steamed green vegetables alongside.

SERVES 2

INGREDIENTS

- I pound new potatoes
- 3 tablespoons vegetable or light olive oil
- 5 sprigs rosemary
- pinch sea salt

METHOD

- Preheat the oven to 350°F.
- Place the new potatoes in a medium saucepan, cover with water, bring to the boil and parboil for 5 minutes.
- Drain the water from the saucepan and set the potatoes aside.
- Pour the oil on a large baking sheet and put in the oven to heat for a few minutes until it is sizzling hot.
- Take the sheet out of the oven and toss the sprigs of rosemary and the potatoes in the oil.
- Sprinkle a pinch of sea salt over the potatoes and mix everything together well. Put the baking sheet back in the oven and roast the potatoes for 30 minutes.

HERBY CROUTONS

SERVES 4

INGREDIENTS

- 4 slices bread (you can use any variety—whole wheat, multigrain, spelt, white, etc.)
- 2 tablespoons light olive oil
- ½ teaspoon sea salt
- I tablespoon mixed herbs (dried or fresh)

METHOD

- Preheat the oven to 325°F.
- Cut the bread into bite-sized cubes and place in a mixing bowl. Drizzle the olive oil and salt over the bread, followed by the herbs, and mix well so that the bread is lightly coated. Spread the coated cubes evenly on a baking sheet and place in the oven. Bake for about 15 minutes until they are golden brown.

PESTO SAUCE

SERVES 4

INGREDIENTS

- I clove garlic, finely chopped
- pinch sea salt
- large handful fresh basil leaves (approx. 4 cups leaves), roughly chopped
- ⅓ cup pine nuts or walnuts, finely chopped
- ½ cup Parmesan cheese or similar hard cheese, finely grated
- 4 tablespoons extra-virgin olive oil

METHOD

- Grind the garlic with a pinch of salt and the basil leaves with a mortar and pestle. Add the pine nuts (or walnuts) and pound again into a paste. Transfer the ingredients to a small mixing bowl and stir in the Parmesan cheese. Then finish by mixing in the olive oil so that the sauce has a gooey consistency.
- If you do not have a mortar and pestle, you can chop the garlic, basil, and pine nuts together on a large chopping board, and then transfer to the mixing bowl. Or, you can blend all the ingredients together in a food processor fitted with a steel blade.

YORKSHIRE PUDDINGS

My husband taught me how to make Yorkshire puddings, and now I am hooked. I like to make them as individual puddings, baked in a non-stick muffin tin, but you can also make one large pudding in a high-sided pan and then cut it into portions. As a child, my dad used to eat them as a sweet dessert—you follow the same recipe, but finish off by pouring warm honey over the top. Comfort food at its best.

SERVES 4 (2 puddings per person)

INGREDIENTS

- ¾ cup all-purpose or light spelt flour
- pinch sea salt
- 2 large, free-range eggs
- 1¼ cups milk
- 8 teaspoons vegetable or light olive oil for the muffin tin

METHOD

- Preheat the oven to 400°F.
- Sift the flour into a medium-sized mixing bowl and add a pinch of salt. Crack the eggs in and whisk together with the flour, then gradually pour in the milk, stirring constantly. Beat all the ingredients together until the batter is the consistency of cream. Refrigerate the batter for 30 minutes.
- Pour 1 teaspoon of oil into the bottom of each of the 8 wells in a non-stick muffin tin. Put the muffin tin in the oven to heat the oil until it's very hot—almost smoking hot (about 5 minutes).
- Give the batter a quick stir and then pour it equally into each well in the tin (you should hear it sizzle and it should bubble). Return the tin to the oven and bake the puddings for 20–25 minutes, until they have risen and are deep golden brown. These are wonderful with Sage and Onion "Roast" (see p. 130), Red Onion Gravy (see p. 171), and jarred, prepared horseradish.

CREAM CHEESE PASTRY

My grandmother taught me how to make this, and I was intrigued to learn that you could make pastry using cream cheese! It can get quite sticky so I think it's best done in a food processor, and it's important to chill the dough in the fridge, once it's mixed, to allow it to firm up. This is a wonderfully indulgent, creamy pastry that works really well for quiches and pies.

MAKES 14 ounces

INGREDIENTS

- 1 stick butter, softened to room temperature
- 4 ounces cream cheese
- 1²⁄₃ cups all-purpose or light spelt flour

METHOD

- If using a food processor: Pulse the butter, cream cheese, and flour in the processor bowl until the dough comes together. Remove from the bowl and gather the dough into a firm ball, flatten it slightly, then wrap it in plastic wrap and refrigerate for about 2 hours, or overnight.
- If mixing by hand: Beat together the butter and cream cheese in a mixing bowl, then add the flour and mix well until the ingredients come together. Using your hands, form the dough into a ball, then wrap in plastic wrap and refrigerate—again, for about 2 hours, or overnight.
- This pastry can be frozen for up to 6 weeks. Let stand at room temperature to defrost completely before rolling out.

BBQ SAUCE

SERVES 6–8

INGREDIENTS

· 2 cups tomato ketchup
· juice of 1 lemon
· 2 tablespoons balsamic vinegar or white wine vinegar
· 4 cloves garlic, finely chopped
· 3 tablespoons mustard, preferably French Dijon
· 1¼ cup vegetable or light olive oil
· sea salt and black pepper, to taste

METHOD

· Mix all the ingredients together in a bowl.
· Either refrigerate for later use or pour the sauce onto a large baking sheet and add burgers, sausages, or chunky-cut vegetables of your choice. Make sure they get well coated with the sauce. Then all you have to do is cook them on your barbecue or under the broiler—and enjoy.

AUNTIE'S CARAWAY COLESLAW

My Aunt Louise's coleslaw recipe is tangy and a bit different. I love my Aunt Louise.

SERVES 4

INGREDIENTS

· 3 cups white cabbage, thinly sliced or grated
· 3 cups red cabbage, thinly sliced or grated (or use 6 cups white cabbage if you don't have any red)
· 1 medium carrot, grated
· 2 teaspoons caraway seeds

For the dressing:
· 2 tablespoons Dijon mustard (grainy or smooth)
· ¼ cup cider vinegar or white wine vinegar
· 5 tablespoons extra-virgin olive oil
· sea salt and black pepper, to taste

METHOD

· Combine the cabbage, carrot, and caraway seeds in a medium salad bowl. Whisk the dressing ingredients together in a small bowl. Drizzle the dressing over the cabbage and carrots, season with sea salt and black pepper, and toss well.

OVEN-BAKED STEAK FRIES

SERVES 4

INGREDIENTS

- 4 large potatoes, such as Yukon Gold or Russet, washed and peeled
- 3 tablespoons vegetable or light olive oil
- large pinch sea salt

METHOD

- Preheat the oven to 400°F. Place 2 large non-stick baking sheets in the oven to heat.
- Cut the potatoes into long strips, about ⅔ inch thick, and put them into a large mixing bowl. Drizzle the oil over the potatoes and toss well to coat fries.
- Take the preheated baking sheets out of oven and lay the fries evenly on them. Sprinkle the sea salt over them and bake in the oven until they're golden brown, about 30 minutes.

RED ONION GRAVY

SERVES 4

INGREDIENTS

- 2 tablespoons vegetable or light olive oil
- 2 medium red onions, thinly sliced
- I tablespoon dried or 2 tablespoons fresh mixed herbs
- 2 tablespoons cornstarch
- 3⅔ cups vegetable stock
- I tablespoon soy sauce
- ⅔ cup red wine (optional)

METHOD

- Heat the oil in a medium, heavy-bottomed saucepan over medium heat, then sauté the onions for about 5 minutes until they've softened. Stir in the herbs.
- Meanwhile, put the cornstarch into a pitcher and slowly whisk in the stock. Then slowly pour this stock into the saucepan with the onions, stirring constantly until all the stock has been added.
- Add the soy sauce and the red wine (if using).
- Simmer gently, stirring often, for about 10–12 minutes, until the gravy has thickened.

RED BEETS IN CRÈME FRAÎCHE

When I first started cooking with red beets I used to peel and boil them and wonder why all the color seeped into the water, leaving the beets looking pale. Then my mum showed me that if you leave the skins on to cook (boil or bake) them, and then peel the beets afterward, they retain their color and flavor.

A little squeeze of lime juice lifts the dish and gives the flavors an extra lightness. This is the perfect side dish to accompany a hotpot or serve with a large chopped salad—or even at a barbecue.

SERVES 2

INGREDIENTS

· I bunch fresh medium red beets (approx. I pound)
· 3 tablespoons crème fraîche or sour cream
· squeeze of fresh lime or lemon juice
· I tablespoon fresh parsley, chopped (optional)
· sea salt and black pepper, to taste

METHOD

· Preheat the oven to 350°F.
· Wash the beets and prick the skin a couple of times with a knife or fork. Bake them, in their skins, for I hour, until cooked through.
· Wait until they're cool enough to handle, but still warm (you don't want to burn your fingers), then peel and thinly slice them and place in a medium mixing bowl.
· Stir in the crème fraîche (or sour cream) and add a squeeze of lime or lemon juice. Mix well, and season with a little sea salt and some freshly ground black pepper. I like to serve this warm, but it can be eaten at room temperature.

SILKY CHOCOLATE SAUCE

This sauce has so many great uses! Drizzle it onto Coconut Rice Pudding on p. 206 or over a banana split! I also love this chocolate sauce simply spooned over vanilla ice cream.

SERVES 4

INGREDIENTS

- 3½ ounces bittersweet chocolate (minimum 70% cocoa solids), or milk chocolate if you prefer
- 4 tablespoons heavy cream

METHOD

- Pour about 2-3 inches of water into a medium saucepan and bring to a gentle simmer over low heat.
- Break the chocolate into chunks and put it into a large heatproof bowl that will sit on top of the saucepan.
- Add the cream to the bowl of chocolate pieces. Rest the bowl over the pan of simmering water, making sure it does not touch the water. Gently heat the chocolate until it is just melted. Stir well and remove from the heat so it doesn't overcook. It should have a silky, glossy consistency.

TOFFEE SAUCE

This salty-sweet sauce is completely delicious spooned over banana splits, as a topping for an ice-cream treat or served warm, drizzled over baked apples, to name but a few options.

SERVES 4

INGREDIENTS

- 1 stick salted butter
- ½ cup packed light brown sugar
- 5 tablespoons maple syrup
- ¾ cup heavy cream

METHOD

- Gently heat the butter, sugar, maple syrup, and cream in a small or medium saucepan until melted together and smooth.

DESSERTS AND BAKING

ORANGE AND LEMON CUPCAKES

I used to make these as vanilla cupcakes, but one day my eldest son requested something a bit different—so I came up with a citrus combination that has become a family favorite. I think the sweetness of the orange cupcakes complements the sharpness of the lemon-flavored icing really well.

MAKES 12

INGREDIENTS

- 1 stick butter, softened to room temperature
- ½ cup superfine sugar
- 2 large, free-range eggs
- 1 cup self-rising flour
- zest and juice of 1 large orange (approx. 3 tablespoons juice)

- 12 paper cupcake liners

For the icing:
- 2 tablespoons butter, softened
- 2 cups confectioner's sugar
- zest and juice of 1 large lemon

METHOD

- Preheat the oven to 350°F. Line a non-stick muffin tin with 12 cupcake liners.
- Either with a wooden spoon in a large mixing bowl or with an electric mixer, cream the butter until it is fluffy, then beat in the sugar. Add the eggs, one at a time, mixing thoroughly. Gradually mix in the flour and beat well until the mixture is light in texture. Stir in the orange zest and juice. Beat together for a few minutes to make sure all is well combined.
- Divide the cupcake batter equally between the 12 cupcake liners.
- Bake for 15–18 minutes, until the cakes are golden on top but still light and springy to the touch. Take them out of the oven and cool.
- To make the lemon icing, put the softened butter into a medium mixing bowl, sift in half of the confectioner's sugar and beat the two together. Stir in the lemon zest and juice, then sift in the remaining confectioner's sugar and beat well. To finish, evenly spread the lemon icing onto each cupcake and they are ready to eat.

MY BROWNIES

I couldn't really write a cookbook without including brownies. My schoolfriends used to love it when Mum made a fresh batch of brownies; these were very American and not that well known in the 70s and 80s in southeast England, although now, of course, they are famous worldwide! There are so, so many extras that you can add to brownies: chopped pecans or walnuts, broken-up pieces of white chocolate, dried cherries, and so on. But I have opted for a very simple recipe, partly because my kids pick out the nuts, and partly because I love them just like this—with whipped cream or vanilla ice cream on the side—for dessert.

MAKES APPROX. 16 BROWNIES

INGREDIENTS

· flour for dusting the pan
· 3½ ounces bittersweet chocolate (minimum 70% cocoa solids), broken up into chunks
· 10 tablespoons butter, at room temperature, plus more for greasing the pan
· 1 cup sugar, preferably raw superfine sugar
· 2 large, free-range eggs, beaten
· 1 teaspoon vanilla extract
· ½ cup self-rising flour

METHOD

· Preheat the oven to 350°F. Butter and lightly flour a non-stick baking pan, about 9 x 9 inches.
· To melt the chocolate, place the broken-up chocolate pieces in a medium heatproof mixing bowl. Rest it on a pan of gently simmering boiling water (the water only needs to be about 1 inch deep). The moment the chocolate has melted take it off the heat and let it cool slightly.
· Meanwhile, in a separate mixing bowl beat the butter until it becomes lighter in color, then add the sugar and beat well until it becomes light and fluffy. Gradually whisk in the beaten eggs and mix well. Stir in the vanilla and the melted chocolate (making sure the chocolate is not too hot, so it doesn't cook the eggs). Mix in the flour and combine well.
· Pour the brownie mixture into the prepared baking pan and bake for 25–30 minutes. Take it out of the oven and cool slightly, then invert the brownies onto a wire cooling rack or plate. The brownies should be moist and a bit gooey. Cut into squares or rectangles, and serve.

ARTY'S CHOCOLATE CHIP COOKIES

My eldest son loves chocolate chip cookies; this recipe is the first he made for me, hence the name. I think they are addictive—once I start munching them I find it hard to stop, and the smell of home-baked cookies is hard to beat. If you want an extra citrus twist to these, you can add the zest of one orange when you're mixing in the chocolate pieces.

MAKES 18–20 COOKIES

INGREDIENTS

· 1 stick salted butter, softened to room temperature
· ⅓ cup raw superfine sugar
· 1 large, free-range egg, beaten
· 1 teaspoon vanilla extract
· ⅔ cup all-purpose or light spelt flour
· ½ teaspoon baking soda
· 6 ounces bittersweet chocolate (minimum 70% cocoa solids), broken up into little chunks (or milk chocolate if you prefer)

METHOD

· Preheat the oven to 375°F. Line a baking sheet with parchment paper—or use a non-stick sheet.
· Cream the butter and sugar together in a large mixing bowl. Mix in the egg and the vanilla and beat well. Then mix in the rest of the ingredients.
· Spoon tablespoons of the cookie dough onto the baking sheet, spacing them out well, so they won't stick together as they expand in the oven, and gently flatten them slightly.
· Bake for about 15 minutes, or until they are lightly golden and just firm to the touch; they will harden up as they cool.
· Transfer the cookies to a wire rack to cool. Then eat!

CHOOSE-YOUR-OWN-FLAVOR LOAF CAKE

It makes me happy to have a loaf cake on display at home, sitting on a glass cake stand. It's so welcoming. And the joy of this is that you can use the basic recipe and then choose the flavor you want, depending on your mood: vanilla, lemon, or chocolate—or whatever you like. For the one in this photo I made a vanilla cake mix and stirred in melted chocolate without mixing it in too much—to give it a marble effect.

SERVES 8

INGREDIENTS

· flour for dusting the pan
· 1¾ sticks butter, at room temperature, plus more for greasing the pan
· 1 cup superfine sugar or granulated sugar
· 3 large, free-range eggs
· 1⅔ cups self-rising flour

Choice of flavors:
· 1 teaspoon vanilla extract
· OR zest and juice of 1 lemon
· OR 3 ounces melted chocolate
· OR zest and juice of 1 orange

METHOD

· Preheat the oven to 350°F. Butter and flour a 9-inch non-stick loaf pan.
· In a large mixing bowl, beat the butter and sugar together until the butter becomes paler and takes on the consistency of thick cream, then gradually beat in the eggs.
· Gently fold in the flour. Add the flavoring of your choice, mixing well, before pouring the cake batter into the loaf pan and smoothing the top with a knife.
· Bake for 50 minutes, until the cake is golden on top and firm and springy to the touch.
· Take the cake out of the oven and let it cool in the pan for about 10 minutes. Then turn it out of the pan onto a wire rack or plate—and it's ready to eat!

LINDA'S LEMON DRIZZLE CAKE

This is a loaf cake that my mum liked to make and it remains a firm favorite of mine. The lemon syrup poured over the freshly baked cake seeps down into the sponge and adds a special moisture to the taste. Perfect to have with a cup of tea in the afternoon.

SERVES 6

INGREDIENTS

- flour for dusting the pan
- I stick butter, softened, plus more for greasing the pan
- ¾ cup superfine sugar
- 2 large, free-range eggs, beaten
- finely grated zest and juice of 3 lemons
- I½ cups all-purpose or light spelt flour
- 2 teaspoons baking powder
- ¼ cup milk
- ½ cup confectioner's sugar, sifted

METHOD

- Preheat the oven to 350°F. Butter and flour a 9-inch non-stick loaf pan.
- In a medium mixing bowl, cream the butter and sugar together with a wooden spoon (or use an electric mixer). Gradually beat in the eggs and mix until light and fluffy. Stir in the lemon zest, flour, and baking powder, and mix well. Add 2 tablespoons of the lemon juice and mix well again. Then beat in the milk.
- Pour the cake batter evenly into the prepared loaf pan and bake for 45 minutes.
- In the meantime, mix the remaining lemon juice and the confectioner's sugar together in a small bowl to make a glaze.
- When it's ready, take the cake out of the oven and cool in the pan for 5 minutes. Then turn it out onto a plate. Pierce the top of the cake all over with a thin skewer. Spoon the lemon glaze carefully and evenly over the cake until all of it is absorbed. Ready to eat.

PEACHES AND CREAM PAVLOVA

My second eldest son loves meringues, so we make this dessert together. It has a wonderful meringue base topped with sweetened vanilla whipped cream and ripe sliced fruit. It also works really well with seasonal ripe peaches or nectarines, but if you can't get a hold of them, you can scatter a mix of fresh berries—such as blueberries, raspberries, and strawberries—on top. Or, to make it more autumnal, sliced ripe pears with toasted pecans and grated chocolate on top works well, too.

SERVES 6

INGREDIENTS

- 4 large, free-range egg whites
- ¼ teaspoon lemon juice
- pinch salt
- 1½ teaspoons vanilla extract
- ½ cup superfine sugar

For the topping:
- 1 cup heavy cream
- 1 tablespoon vanilla extract
- 3 peaches or nectarines, halved, pitted, and thinly sliced

METHOD

- Preheat the oven to 275°F. Line a large baking sheet with parchment paper.
- With an electric mixer, beat the egg whites until they are light, airy, and nearly stiff. Add the lemon juice, salt, and the 1½ teaspoons of vanilla, and continue beating at medium speed while adding the sugar a little at a time.
- Spoon this meringue mixture onto the baking sheet and spread it out to form a round base, about 6-7 inches wide.
- Bake in the oven for 1½ hours, or until the outer part of the meringue is crisp. Turn off the heat and leave it in the oven for ½ hour. Then take the baking sheet out of the oven and slide the meringue gently onto the serving plate.
- In the meantime, prepare the cream and fruit topping. Whip the cream until it just stiffens and holds its shape, and then mix in the vanilla. You do not want to over-whip the cream.
- Smooth the whipped cream evenly over the top of the cooled meringue. Then decorate with the peaches or nectarines in a design spiraling out from the center. Ready to serve.

MAPLE SYRUP BAKED PEACHES AND APRICOTS

This is a yummy summer dessert when peaches and apricots are in season. If you can't find both ripe at the same time, just use either peaches or apricots. It makes for a sweet, light dessert that I think works well after an indulgent meal.

SERVES 6

INGREDIENTS

· 6 ripe peaches
· 12 ripe apricots
· 2 tablespoons butter, finely diced
· 6 tablespoons maple syrup
· 2 teaspoons fresh thyme leaves, chopped

METHOD

· Preheat the oven to 350°F. Line a baking sheet with aluminum foil or parchment paper.
· Slice the peaches in half and take out the pits, then do the same with the apricots. Arrange the fruit, hollow side up, on the baking sheet. Divide the butter evenly between the hollowed-out peach and apricot halves.
· Drizzle the maple syrup over the fruit and sprinkle the fresh thyme on top.
· Bake in the oven for 25 minutes, until bubbling hot and turning golden. This is heaven served with vanilla ice cream, with cream poured over the top, or simply on their own!

PLUM AND PEAR CRUMBLE

Crumble is delicious and I like to think of it as deceptively guilt-free. It packs a whopping fruity punch and is also very versatile. You can play around with the fruit combinations, using apples and blackberries instead, or berries, depending on what is in season. This dessert can be served on its own, but is also great with custard, whipped cream, or ice cream.

SERVES 4

INGREDIENTS

For the filling:
- 8 ripe plums, cut in half and pitted
- 4 ripe but firm pears, cored and cut lengthwise into quarters
- ½ cup packed light brown sugar
- I teaspoon ground cinnamon

For the crumble:
- ⅔ cup all-purpose flour
- I cup rolled oats
- ½ cup ground almonds
- ¼ cup packed light brown sugar
- 7 tablespoons butter, chilled and cut into cubes

METHOD

- Preheat the oven to 375°F.
- Cut the sliced plums and pears into bite-sized pieces and put them into a medium baking dish (about 10 inches). Sprinkle the brown sugar and the cinnamon evenly over the fruit and stir together well.
- To make the crumble, put the flour, oats, ground almonds, and brown sugar into a medium mixing bowl. Then add the butter and gently rub these ingredients together using your fingertips, until the mixture resembles coarse breadcrumbs.
- Scatter the crumble evenly over the prepared fruit in the baking dish.
- Bake for 45 minutes, until the topping is golden and crisp, and serve warm or at room temperature.

CREAMY CHOCOLATE MOUSSE

This rich mousse is great for a dinner party dessert, with quite a "grown-up" dark chocolate edge to it. The whipped cream in the recipe adds lightness to the mousse. And of course, you could use a good-quality milk chocolate instead, to make it less "grown up!"

SERVES 4

INGREDIENTS

· 5 ounces bittersweet chocolate (minimum 70% cocoa solids), broken up into chunks
· 2 tablespoons butter
· 2 large, free-range eggs
· I tablespoon sugar
· ⅔ cup heavy cream
· ½ teaspoon vanilla extract

METHOD

· Melt the chocolate and butter together in a medium stainless-steel or heat-resistant glass bowl set over a pan half-full of gently simmering water. Stir occasionally and once the mixture has melted, take the bowl off the heat and allow it to cool slightly until just warm.
· Separate the eggs, setting aside the 2 yolks in a small bowl or cup, and then whisk the egg whites and sugar together with an electric mixer or handheld whisk until they have set to a foamy consistency that can form soft peaks.
· In another bowl whip the cream until it too just forms soft peaks, and then whisk in the vanilla extract.
· Once the melted chocolate has had a chance to cool slightly, thoroughly stir in the egg yolks. Now stir in 2 dollops of the whisked egg whites to allow the mix to become smoother, and then gently fold in the rest of the egg whites. Fold, rather than beat them in, as you do not want to knock the bubbles and air out of the mix.
· Finally, lightly fold in the whipped cream and divide the mousse equally between 4 ramekins, small bowls, or pretty teacups. Cover in plastic wrap and refrigerate for at least I hour.
· I like to take the mousse out of the fridge half an hour to I hour before serving to give it a chance to come to room temperature again.

COCONUT RICE PUDDING WITH CHOCOLATE SAUCE

Rice pudding has always been a family favorite. We used to love it when Dad told us the story of how Mum learned how to make baked rice pudding. When they were newlyweds, she kept asking what his favorite dishes were. He mentioned rice pudding. Mum had never made it before and she found a very complicated recipe that was a complete failure—she was so disappointed. So my dad called up our Auntie Jinny in Liverpool and she talked Mum through how easy and tasty it could be. We all loved it.

I cook this rice pudding in a saucepan on the stovetop, and the hint of coconut makes it feel delicately exotic. The dried coconut is an optional extra—I think it gives the pudding a nice texture, but the rice has a creamy smoothness that is just as satisfying without it. The swirl of chocolate sauce on top transforms it into a good dinner party dessert.

SERVES 4

INGREDIENTS

- ½ cup Arborio or short-grain rice
- 14.5 ounce can coconut milk
- 2 tablespoons water
- ¼ cup raw superfine sugar
- I teaspoon vanilla extract
- 2 tablespoons dessicated coconut (optional)
- chocolate sauce, to serve (see p. 175)

METHOD

- Place the rice in a large, heavy-bottomed saucepan. Pour in the coconut milk, then rinse out the can with the 2 tablespoons of water and add it to the pan too.
- Bring to a gentle simmer over medium-low heat, stirring well, and then add the sugar, vanilla extract, and coconut. Now simmer gently, stirring often, for about I5 minutes, until the rice is just cooked through.
- Serve with a drizzle of chocolate sauce on top.

ICE CREAM CELEBRATION CAKE

This is my favorite cake to make for birthdays. I buy the pound cakes, but if you want you can make your own, by following the cake recipe on p. 193, and using the vanilla flavor option. It's a surprising cake, because it is iced, so it looks like a normal frosted cake until you cut into it and see the ice cream center. Kids and grown-ups alike devour it.

MAKES ENOUGH FOR 8 PEOPLE

INGREDIENTS

· 2 9-inch butter pound cakes, store-bought is fine or homemade (see p. 193)
· 2 pints ice cream, mixed flavors, such as vanilla, chocolate, or strawberry (or use all one flavor)

For the icing:
· 10 tablespoons butter, softened to room temperature
· 3¾ cups confectioner's sugar, sifted
· ¼ cup room temperature milk or warm water
· 1 teaspoon vanilla extract
· Decorating sprinkles, or other cake decorations of your choice

METHOD

· Line the bottom and sides of an 8 or 9-inch round, deep, non-stick cake pan with parchment paper. Cut the pound cakes crosswise into slices about ⅔ inch thick. Then completely line the cake pan with the cake slices, slightly overlapping them so there are no gaps (make sure you leave aside some cake slices to lay over the top of the cake later). Using your hands, push the cake down into the sides of the pan.
· Allow the ice cream to soften so that it is easy to scoop out of the cartons. Spoon the ice cream, one flavor at a time, into the prepared cake-lined pan. Use a spoon to press the ice cream down so there are no air pockets. Repeat until the cake pan is filled with ice cream. Then layer the reserved cake slices over the top of the ice cream and press them down firmly. Place a plate over the top of the cake, then put it in the freezer to allow the ice cream to fully freeze again—at least 1 hour, but you can leave it overnight.
· To make the icing, put the butter into a large mixing bowl, then gradually beat in the confectioner's sugar, mix in the milk or warm water, and add the vanilla extract. Beat together well until the icing is light and fluffy.
· When the ice cream has frozen hard again, take the cake out of the freezer and turn the cake pan over onto a plate. Peel away the parchment and spread the icing evenly over the cake, then put the cake back in the freezer until you are ready to serve it.

NUTTY SWEET PIE

This is a tasty variation on a traditional pecan pie—which I love—but this makes a nice change and is delicious served with whipped cream on the side, or a scoop of vanilla ice cream melting on top. For the crust, you can use my Shortcrust Pie Pastry recipe on p. 166, and the golden, nutty filling is quick to throw together.

SERVES 8–10

INGREDIENTS

- 10 ounces Shortcrust Pie Pastry, (see p. 166) or 1 store-bought refrigerated ready-to-roll crust
- flour, for dusting work surface
- 1 stick butter
- 2 tablespoons golden syrup or corn syrup
- ½ cup packed light brown sugar
- 1 teaspoon vanilla extract
- 2⅔ cups mixed nuts (such as Brazils, walnuts, pecans, almonds, hazelnuts), coarsely chopped
- 2 large, free-range eggs, lightly beaten

METHOD

- Preheat the oven to 350°F. Get out a metal pie dish (or use a 9-inch fluted metal removable-bottom tart pan).
- Roll out the pastry on a clean, floured surface to a thickness of about ⅛ inch, slightly larger than the pan. Drape it over the rolling pin and then lay it carefully into the pan. Press the dough into the corners, trim off the excess pastry, and then chill the pie crust in the fridge for half an hour. Line the bottom of the pastry shell with parchment paper and pour in some baking beans or rice (for blind baking the pastry). Bake the pastry shell for about 10 minutes in the middle to lower part of the oven. Then remove the baking beans or rice and parchment paper, and bake the pastry for 10 minutes more, or until it is a light golden color. Take it out of the oven and set aside to cool.
- In a medium saucepan melt the butter and golden syrup together. Turn off the heat, then mix in the brown sugar and the vanilla extract. Add the nuts and mix well so they are well-coated in the sugary melted butter. Allow the mixture to cool slightly, then stir in the beaten eggs. Mix well, then pour the filling into the cooled pastry shell.
- Bake for about 35 minutes, until the crust is golden brown and the filling has set, but is still a little soft. Let the pie cool a little before serving.

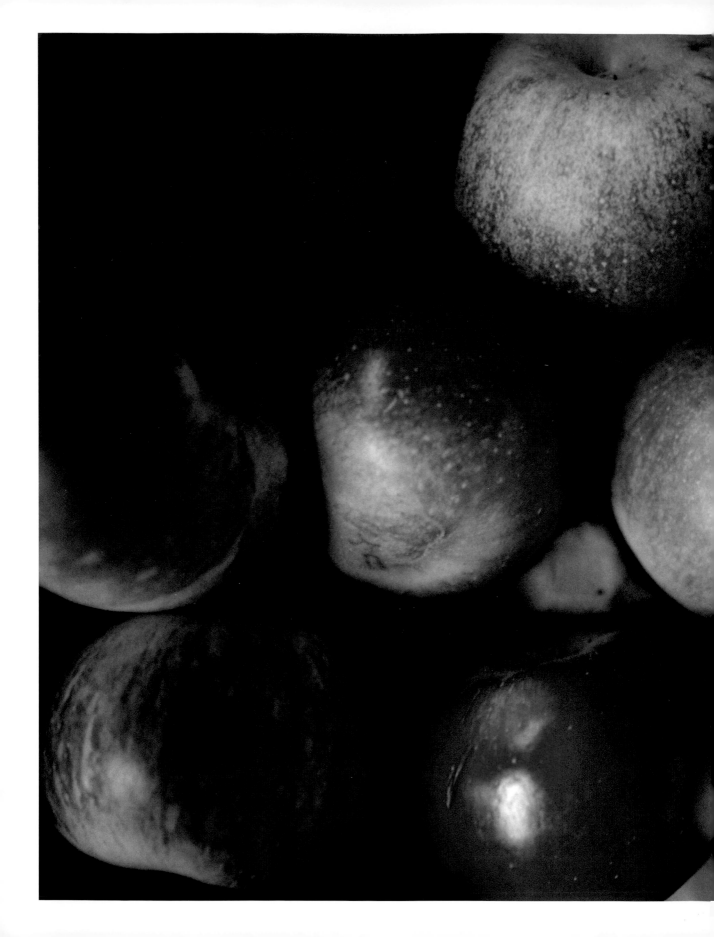

DELICATE
APPLE TART

My step-grandmother first showed me this recipe when I was in my early teens, and I still love to make it today. I think of this tart as quite graceful; it doesn't need to try too hard. The ingredients are few, but the taste is wonderful.

SERVES 6

INGREDIENTS

For the pastry:
· 2 ⅓ cups all-purpose or light spelt flour
· 1½ sticks unsalted butter, chilled and cut into cubes
· a little butter, at room temperature, for the pan
· ¼ teaspoon sea salt
· 4–5 tablespoons cold water

For the filling:
· 4 or 5 apples (use crisp eating apples, not cooking apples)
· 3 tablespoons salted butter
· 3 tablespoons superfine sugar, preferably unrefined (raw)
· ⅓ cup apricot jam (I use St. Dalfour jam)
· 1 tablespoon water

METHOD

· To make the pastry, put the flour, chilled and cubed butter, and the salt into a medium mixing bowl and mix with a spoon or knife until all of the butter is coated with flour.
· Add the water and mix with your fingertips, kneading just until the mixture comes together to form a ball. Take care not to overwork it; pieces of butter should be visible in the pastry (and will give it a wonderful flakiness). Wrap the pastry in plastic wrap and refrigerate for at least 1 hour.
· Preheat the oven to 325°F. Butter a large, thin baking sheet, measuring about 11 x 15 inches.
· On a clean, lightly floured surface, roll out the pastry to a thickness of about ⅛ inch, to the shape of the baking sheet. Gently wrap the pastry around the rolling pin and unroll it onto the sheet pan. Keep it cool in the fridge while you prepare the apples.
· Peel and quarter the apples, core them and then slice them thinly. Arrange the thin apple slices on the pastry in a neat, overlapping design (like the pattern of tiles on a roof), leaving a 2-inch border around the edges, then fold the pastry edges in over the apples to form a frame.
· Dot the butter evenly over the top and then sprinkle sugar evenly over the apples.
· Bake for 60–75 minutes, until the pastry is golden brown and crisp and the apples are browned.
· In a small saucepan melt the apricot jam over low heat with 1 tablespoon of water mixed in, then brush it over the apples. Ready to serve.

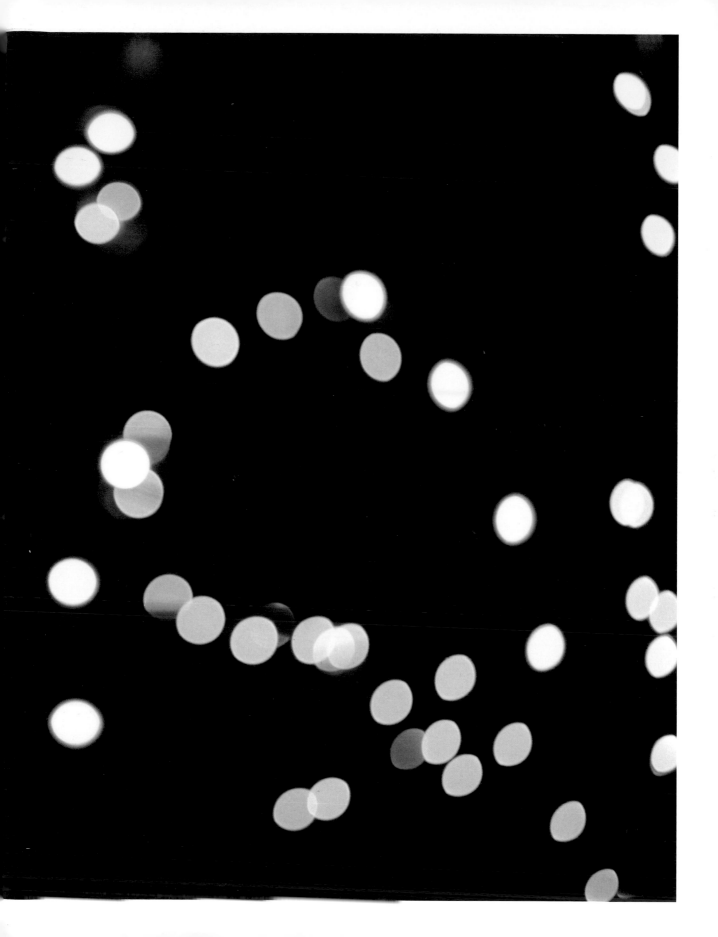

ACKNOWLEDGMENTS

I would like to say a big thank you to Sam, Caroline, and Sha for their invaluable help and patience. For Mum for the memories that made this book possible and Simon for nagging me to do it. Thanks to Dad, Arthur, Elliot, Sam, Sid, Hettie, Stella, and James. To my cousin, Lee, for his advice. To Olivia for the use of her wonder garden, to Gillian at Judith Michaels and Daughter for lending me crockery for photos, to Mark for putting me in touch with a great publishing team. To Sean for the lovely prints. To Aunt Louise and Maxine for ideas, and to Kasia, Brown and Michelle.

INDEX

ALFALFA SPROUTS
· sprout and carrot salad   85
APPLES
· delicate apple tart   215
APRICOTS
· maple syrup baked peaches and apricots   201
ARTY'S CHOCOLATE CHIP COOKIES   190
ASPARAGUS
· asparagus summer tart   117
· new potato and asparagus salad with
  mustard dressing   104
AUNTIE'S CARAWAY COLESLAW   168
AVOCADOS
· avocado salad   84
· guacamole   53
· hummus, avocado and chili jam sandwich   40
· pan-fried tortilla sandwich   41

BALSAMIC ROASTED SHALLOT SALAD   99
BANANAS
· banana muffins   19
· strawberry and banana smoothie   13
BARBECUE (BBQ) SAUCE   168
BEANS
· black bean, corn and feta tacos   121
· hearty quinoa and white bean soup   64
· Mexican bean tortilla   113
see also butter beans
BLACK BEAN, SWEET CORN AND FETA TACOS   121
BLIND BAKING   1
BREAKFAST PANCAKES   27
BROWNIES   187
BUTTERED ZUCCHINI AND CHEESY POLENTA   122
BUTTERNUT SQUASH
· roasted butternut squash and rosemary soup   63

CABBAGE
· Auntie's caraway coleslaw   168
CAKES
· choose-your-own-flavor loaf cake   193
· ice cream celebration cake   209
· Linda's lemon drizzle cake   194
· orange and lemon cupcakes   184
CANNELLINI BEANS
· hearty quinoa and white bean soup   64
CARROTS
· sprout and carrot salad   85
CAULIFLOWER CHEESE   141
CHEESE
· black bean, sweet corn and feta tacos   121
· buttered zucchini and cheesy polenta   122
· cauliflower cheese   141
· cheese and eggplant oven bake   110
· cheesy quiche   114
· cream cheese pastry   164
· haloumi and roasted red pepper salad   94
· haloumi BBQ skewers   50
· jalapeño tostada   54
· lentil and feta salad   93
· mac & cheese with crispy topping   137
· mixed greens, blue cheese and red grape salad   100
· pan-fried cheese, tomato and onion sandwich   42
· pan-fried tortilla sandwich   41
· vegetarian   1
· watercress, radish and feta salad   90
CHOCOLATE   2
· Arty's chocolate chip cookies   190
· brownies   187
· creamy chocolate mousse   205
· loaf cake   193
· silky chocolate sauce   175

CHOOSE-YOUR-OWN-FLAVOR LOAF CAKE   193
COCONUT RICE PUDDING WITH CHOCOLATE
SAUCE   206
COLESLAW
· Auntie's caraway coleslaw   168
COOKIES
· Arty's chocolate chip cookies   190
CORN
· black bean, sweet corn and feta tacos   121
· corn fritters   82
CORN FRITTERS   82
CREAM CHEESE PASTRY   164
CREAMY CHOCOLATE MOUSSE   205
CROUTONS, HERBY   160
CRUMBLE
· plum and pear crumble   202

DELICATE APPLE TART   215
DELUXE EGG SALAD   49

EASY-PEASY SOUP   70
EGGS   2
· breakfast pancakes   27
· deep-filled omelette   31
· deluxe egg salad   49
· French toast   20
EGGPLANT
· cheese and eggplant oven bake   110
· eggplant wraps   81
· warm eggplant sandwich   46

FREEZING FOOD   1
FRENCH TOAST   20
FRITTATA
· spinach, leek and zucchini frittata   119
FRUIT AND NUT GRANOLA   10
FRUIT, FRESH

· maple syrup baked peaches and apricots   201
· mixed greens, blue cheese and red grape salad   100
· peaches and cream pavlova   197
· plum and pear crumble   202
· rhubarb compote   24
· strawberry and banana smoothie   13
· tropical pineapple and coconut smoothie   13

GRANOLA
· fruit and nut granola   10
· quick breakfast bowl   19
· granola bar to go   16
GRAPES
· mixed greens, blue cheese and red grape salad   100
GRAVY
· red onion gravy   171
· white bean gravy stew   118
GUACAMOLE   53

HALOUMI AND ROASTED RED PEPPER SALAD   94
HALOUMI BBQ SKEWERS   50
HEARTY QUINOA AND WHITE BEAN SOUP   64
HERBY   160
HUMMUS, AVOCADO AND CHILI JAM
SANDWICH   40

ICE CREAM CELEBRATION CAKE   209

JALAPEÑO TOSTADA   54

LASAGNA
· mushroom and leek   138–9
LEEKS
· leek and pea risotto   125
· leek, zucchini and white bean soup   78
· mushroom and leek lasagna   138–9
· spinach, leek and zucchini frittata   119

LEMONS
· Linda's lemon drizzle cake   194
· loaf cake   193
· orange and lemon cupcakes   184
LENTILS
· lentil and feta salad   93
· lightning lentil soup   77
LIGHTNING LENTIL SOUP   77
LINDA'S LEMON DRIZZLE CAKE   194
LIP-SMACKING MINESTRONE   73

MAC & CHEESE WITH CRISPY TOPPING   137
MAPLE SYRUP BAKED PEACHES AND APRICOTS   201
MERINGUE
· peaches and cream pavlova   197
MEXICAN BEAN TORTILLA   113
MINESTRONE   73
MIXED GREENS, BLUE CHEESE AND RED GRAPE
SALAD   100
MOUSSE
· creamy chocolate mousse   205
MUESLI
· quick breakfast bowl   19
MUFFINS, BANANA   19
MUSHROOMS
· deep-filled omelette   31
· mushroom and leek lasagna   138–9
· one-pot mushroom rice   126
· saucy mushrooms and tomatoes on toast   28
MUST-HAVE CREAMY TOMATO SOUP   76

NOODLES
· yummy spicy rice noodles   142
NUTTY SWEET PIE   210

OATS   see porridge oats
ONE-POT MUSHROOM RICE   126

ONIONS
· red onion gravy   171
· sage and onion "roast"   130
ORANGES
· loaf cake   193
· orange and lemon cupcakes   184
OVEN-BAKED STEAK FRIES   171

PAN-FRIED CHEESE, TOMATO AND ONION
SANDWICH   42
PAN-FRIED TORTILLA SANDWICH   41
PANCAKES, BREAKFAST   27
PASTA   1
· zucchini and lemon spaghetti   145
· mac & cheese with crispy topping   137
PASTA SAUCES
· tomato and red wine   146
· white spaghetti   136
PASTRY
· cream cheese pastry   164
· shortcrust pie pastry   166
PAVLOVA
· peaches and cream pavlova   197
PEACHES
· maple syrup baked peaches and apricots   201
· peaches and cream pavlova   197
PEARS
· plum and pear crumble   202
PEAS
· easy-peasy soup   70
· leek and pea risotto   125
PEPPERS
· haloumi and roasted red pepper salad   94
· pesto sauce   160
PINEAPPLE
· tropical pineapple and coconut smoothie   13
PLUM AND PEAR CRUMBLE   202

POLENTA
· buttered zucchini and cheesy polenta 122
POPCORN 47
PORRIDGE OATS
· granola bar to go 16
· hearty porridge 24
POTATOES
· new potato and asparagus salad with mustard
  dressing 104
· oven-baked steak fries 171
· roasted rosemary new potatoes 159
· shepherd's pie 134
· winter warmer hotpot 133

QUICHE, CHEESY 114
QUICK BREAKFAST BOWL 19
QUINOA
· hearty quinoa and white bean soup 64
· super quinoa salad 103

RADISHES
· watercress, radish and feta salad 90
· rhubarb compote 24
RED BEETS IN CRÈME FRAÎCHE 172
RICE
· coconut rice pudding with chocolate sauce 206
· leek and pea risotto 125
· one-pot mushroom rice 126
RISOTTO
· leek and pea risotto 125
· roasted rosemary new potatoes 159

SAGE AND ONION "ROAST" 130
SALADS
· avocado 84
· balsamic roasted shallot 99
· deluxe egg salad 49

· haloumi and roasted red pepper 94
· lentil and feta 93
· mixed greens, blue cheese and red grape 100
· new potato and asparagus, with mustard
  dressing 104
· quinoa 103
· sprout and carrot 85
· watercress, radish and feta 90
SANDWICHES
· deluxe egg salad 49
· hummus, avocado and chili jam 40
· pan-fried cheese, tomato and onion 42
· pan-fried tortilla 41
· warm eggplant sandwich 46
SAUCES
· barbecue (BBQ) 168
· chocolate 175
· pesto 160
· toffee 175
· tomato and red wine (for pasta) 146
· white spaghetti 136
SAUCY MUSHROOMS AND TOMATOES ON TOAST 28
SAUSAGES, VEGETARIAN 2
· winter warmer hotpot 133
SHALLOTS
· balsamic roasted shallot salad 99
SHEPHERD'S PIE 134
SHORTCRUST PIE PASTRY 166
SILKY CHOCOLATE SAUCE 175
SMOOTHIES
· strawberry and banana 13
· tropical pineapple and coconut 13
SOUPS
· butternut squash and rosemary 63
· easy-peasy 70
· leek, zucchini and white bean 78
· lentil 77

· lip-smacking minestrone   73
· quinoa and white bean   64
· tomato   76
SPELT FLOUR, LIGHT   3
SPINACH
· eggplant wraps   81
· spinach, leek and zucchini frittata   119
STEAK FRIES, OVEN-BAKED   171
STOCKS, VEGETABLE   2, 167
STRAWBERRY AND BANANA SMOOTHIE   13
SUGAR   2

TACOS
· black bean, sweet corn and feta   121
TARTS
· asparagus summer tart   117
· delicate apple tart   215
TOFFEE SAUCE   175
TOMATOES
· deep-filled omelette   31
· must-have creamy tomato soup   76
· pan-fried cheese, tomato and onion sandwich   42
· saucy mushrooms and tomatoes on toast   28
· tomato and red wine sauce   146
TORTILLAS
· jalapeño tostada   54
· Mexican bean tortilla   113
· pan-fried tortilla sandwich   41
TROPICAL PINEAPPLE AND COCONUT SMOOTHIE   13

VANILLA EXTRACT   2
· loaf cake   193
VEGETABLE STOCK   2, 167
VEGETABLES, MIXED
· minestrone   73
· shepherd's pie   134
· yummy spicy rice noodles   142
see also specific vegetables

WATERCRESS
· mixed greens, blue cheese and red grape salad   100
· watercress, radish and feta salad   90
WHITE BEANS
· white bean gravy stew   118
· leek, zucchini and white bean soup   78
· winter warmer hotpot   133
WINTER WARMER HOTPOT   133

YORKSHIRE PUDDINGS   163
YUMMY SPICY RICE NOODLES   142

ZUCCHINI
· buttered zucchini and cheesy polenta   122
· leek, zucchini and white bean soup   78
· spinach, leek and zucchini frittata   119
· zucchini and lemon spaghetti   145

For my family, for eating, talking, laughing, and inspiring.